SECOND EDITION

NEW PASSWORD 4
A READING AND VOCABULARY TEXT

Linda Butler
Holyoke Community College

PEARSON
Longman

Dedicato ai miei amici in Italia con un abbraccio

New Password 4: A Reading and Vocabulary Text

Pearson Education, 10 Bank Street, White Plains, NY 10606

Staff credits: The people who made up the *New Password 4* team, representing editorial, production, design, and manufacturing, are: Pietro Alongi, Rhea Banker, Dave Dickey, Jaime Lieber, Maria Pia Marrella, Amy McCormick, Linda Moser, Carlos Rountree, Jennifer Stem, and Paula Van Ells.

Development editor: Thomas Ormond
Project editor: Helen B. Ambrosio
Text design & composition: ElectraGraphics, Inc.
Cover design: Maria Pia Marrella
Cover photos: iStockphoto.com; Image Source/Corbis
Illustrations: Susan Tait Porcaro, Wendy Duran

Text credits, photography credits, references, and acknowledgments appear on page xii.

Library of Congress Cataloging-in-Publication Data
Butler, Linda,
  New password 4 : a reading and vocabulary text / Linda Butler. — 1st ed.
    p. cm.
  Includes bibliographical references and index.
  ISBN-13: 978-0-13-246305-8 (with audio)
  ISBN-10: 0-13-246305-9 (with audio)
  ISBN-13: 978-0-13-246304-1 (without audio)
  ISBN-10: 0-13-246304-0 (without audio)
1. English language—Textbooks for foreign speakers. 2. Vocabulary—Problems, exercises, etc. 3. Readers. I. Title. II. Title: New password four.
  PE1128.B861393 2010
  428.0076—dc22
                                                    2009027401

PEARSON LONGMAN ON THE **WEB**

Pearsonlongman.com offers online resources for teachers and students. Access our Companion Websites, our online catalog, and our local offices around the world.

Visit us at **pearsonlongman.com**.

Printed in the United States of America
ISBN-13: 978-0-13-246304-1   1 2 3 4 5 6 7 8 9 10—DWL— 15 14 13 12 11 10 09
ISBN-13: 978-0-13-246305-8   1 2 3 4 5 6 7 8 9 10—DWL— 15 14 13 12 11 10 09

CONTENTS

SCOPE AND SEQUENCE

	Developing Reading Skills	Developing Other Language Skills	Target Vocabulary
Chapter 7 **Tears**	• Quoting to answer comprehension questions • Recognizing the better paraphrase; using paraphrases	• Sharing opinions • Writing a paragraph on a choice of topics related to crying • Studying Collocations: *View*	*blink, blow, chemical, differ, emotional, fill in, flow, go ahead, liquid, material, mental, normal, surface, throughout, view*
Chapter 8 **Bionic Men and Women**	• Quoting and paraphrasing in answers to comprehension questions • Text organization • Writing a summary	• Role-play • Writing a paragraph on a choice of topics • Studying Collocations: Word pairs with prepositions	*artificial, attach, battery, beat, chest, demand, development, engineer, keep up with, key, regularly, replace, strength, therefore, within*
UNIT 2: Wrap-up	• Review of the target vocabulary • Expanding Vocabulary: Transitive and intransitive verbs • Building Dictionary Skills: Understanding codes		

UNIT 3: Exploring Technology

	Developing Reading Skills	Developing Other Language Skills	Target Vocabulary
Chapter 9 **A History of Telling Time**	• Text organization • Scanning • Understanding reference words	• Discussion • Writing a paragraph on a choice of topics related to time • Word Grammar: The root *port*	*accurate, attend, constant, container, drip, equal, event, fairly, high-tech, measure, modern, portable, shadow, technology, transportation*
Chapter 10 **Out with the Old, In with the New?**	• Comparing and contrasting • Understanding inference • Summarizing	• Sharing opinions • Writing a paragraph on changes in traditions or technology • Word Grammar: *Rob* vs. *steal*	*annoyed, blame, complex, conflict, deserve, fill out, improve, loss, make fun of, matter, multiply, rob, subtract, valuable, vary*
Chapter 11 **Appropriate Technologies**	• Problem and solution • Cause and effect • Supporting details	• Discussion • Writing a paragraph on technology or working in a developing country • Word Grammar: *Technology* as count and noncount noun	*appropriate, be better off, grain, load, method, model, plenty, pollution, production, repair, rural, screen, solution, solve, the environment*
Chapter 12 **Technology in Science Fiction**	• Paraphrasing • Using context clues • Summarizing	• Sharing opinions • Writing a paragraph on a choice of topics related to your own life and science fiction • Word Grammar: *In spite of*	*adventure, century, confused, criminal, description, imagination, in spite of, make up, neither . . . nor, outer space, predict, scientific, society, style, take off*

	Developing Reading Skills	Developing Other Language Skills	Target Vocabulary
UNIT 3: Wrap-up	• Review of the target vocabulary • Expanding Vocabulary: Antonyms and adjectives • Building Dictionary Skills: Words with multiple meanings		
UNIT 4: The Environment			
Chapter 13 **Small Ride, Big Trouble**	• Cause and effect • Problem and solution • The writer's point of view	• Discussion • Writing a paragraph on pollution • Word Grammar: *Loan, lend, borrow*	*association, border, competition, decrease, engine, estimate, fuel, harm, income, interest, loan, maintain, meanwhile, passenger, vehicle*
Chapter 14 **Your Trees, My Trees, Our Trees**	• Recognizing and writing about topics of paragraphs • Fact vs. opinion	• Sharing opinions • Writing a paragraph on a statistic from the reading or on feeling grateful • Studying Collocations: *Resources*	*benefit, carbon dioxide, diameter, flood, grateful, ink, look into, oxygen, population, renewable, resource, rubber, shade, soil, urban*
Chapter 15 **Would You Eat Bugs to Save the World?**	• Main ideas, major points, and supporting details • Comparing and contrasting	• Discussion • Writing a paragraph about eating insects or about speaking out • Word Grammar: *Unless*	*be in favor of, be open to, current, educate, environmental, expert, force, in terms of, protein, raise, require, set out, source, speak out, unless*
Chapter 16 **A Small Creature with a Big Job**	• Text organization • Main ideas, major points, and supporting details • The writer's point of view	• Discussion • Writing a paragraph about yourself • Word Grammar: *Occur (to), happen, take place*	*agriculture, at least, call on, crisis, crop, essential, hunt, immediately, lie, motor, occur, pesticide, productive, threat, yet*
UNIT 4: Wrap-up	• Review of the target vocabulary • Expanding Vocabulary: Word families • Building Dictionary Skills: Words with multiple meanings		
UNIT 5: Economics			
Chapter 17 **Economics—What's It All About?**	• Cause and effect • Understanding the writer's purpose	• Discussion • Writing a paragraph about cost-benefit analyses • Word Grammar: *Economics* + singular verb; *economic(al)*	*approach, debt, economics, exchange, individual, involve, labor, necessary, opportunity, property, rise, scarce, since, take into account, the economy*

THE SECOND EDITION OF THE *PASSWORD* SERIES

Welcome to *New Password,* the second edition of *Password,* a series designed to help learners of English develop their reading skills and expand their vocabularies. The series offers theme-based units consisting of

- engaging nonfiction reading passages,
- a variety of skill-development activities based on the passages, and
- exercises to help students understand, remember, and use new words.

With this new edition, the *Password* series expands from three levels to five. Each book can be used independently of the others, but when used as a series, the books will help students reach the 2,000-word vocabulary level in English, at which point, research has shown, most learners can begin to read unadapted texts.

The series is based on two central ideas. The first is that the best way for learners to develop their ability to read English is, as you might guess, to practice reading English. To spark and sustain the student's motivation to read, "second language reading instruction must find ways to avoid continually frustrating the reader."[1] Learners need satisfying reading materials at an appropriate level of difficulty, materials that do not make them feel as if they are struggling to decipher a puzzle. The level of difficulty is determined by many factors, but one key factor is the familiarity of the vocabulary. Note that

> There is now a large body of studies indicating that poor readers primarily differ from good readers in context-free word recognition, and not in deficiencies in ability to use context to form predictions.[2]

To be successful, readers must be able to recognize a great many words quickly. So in addition to providing engaging reading matter, the *Password* series carefully controls and recycles the vocabulary.

The second idea underlying the design of the series is that textbooks should teach the vocabulary that will be most useful to learners. Corpus-based research has shown that the 2,000 highest-frequency words in English account for almost 80 percent of the running words in academic texts.[3] These are thus highly valuable words for students to learn, and these are the words targeted in the *Password* series.

The chart below shows the number of words that each *New Password* book assumes will be familiar to the learner and the range of the high-frequency vocabulary targeted in the book.

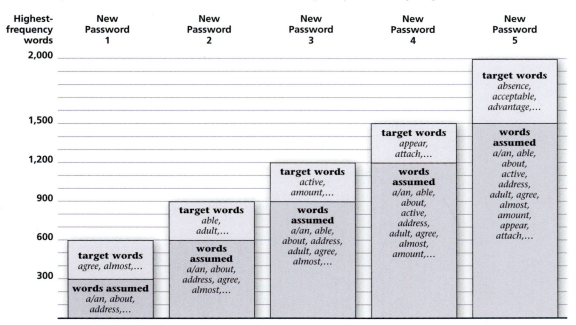

[1]Thom Hudson, *Teaching Second Language Reading* (Oxford, UK: Oxford University Press, 2007) 291.
[2]C. Juel, quoted in *Teaching and Researching Reading*, William Grabe and Fredericka Stoller (Harlow, England: Pearson Education, 2002) 73.
[3]I. S. P. Nation, *Learning Vocabulary in Another Language* (Cambridge, England: Cambridge University Press, 2001) 17.

Target word choices are based on analyses of authentic language data in various corpora, including data in the Longman Corpus Network, to determine which words are most frequently used and most likely to be needed by the learner. Also targeted are common collocations and other multiword units, such as phrasal verbs.[4] The target vocabulary is chosen most often for its usefulness across a range of subjects but occasionally for its value in dealing with the topic of one particular chapter. Other factors include the complexity of a word's meanings and uses.

While becoming a good reader in English involves much more than knowing the meanings of words, there is no doubt that vocabulary knowledge is essential. To learn new words, students need to see them repeatedly and in varied contexts. They must become skilled at guessing meaning from context but can do this successfully only when they understand the context. Research by Paul Nation and Liu Na suggests that "for successful guessing [of unknown words] . . . at least 95 percent of the words in the text must be familiar to the reader."[5] For that reason, the vocabulary in the readings has been carefully controlled so that unknown words should constitute no more than 5 percent of the text. The words used in a reading are limited to those high-frequency words that the learner is assumed to know plus the vocabulary targeted in the chapter and target words and phrases recycled from previous chapters. New vocabulary is explained and practiced, encountered again in later chapters, and reviewed in the Unit

Wrap-ups and Vocabulary Self-Tests. This emphasis on systematic vocabulary acquisition is a highlight of the *Password* series.

The second edition has expanded the series from three levels to five, increasing the number of reading passages from 76 to 104 and expanding the coverage of high-frequency vocabulary. One completely new book has joined the series, the beginning-level *New Password 1*. *New Password 2, 3, 4,* and *5* have retained the most popular materials from the first edition of the series and added new chapters. The books vary somewhat in organization and content, to meet the diverse needs of beginning- to high-intermediate-level students, but all five feature the popular Unit Wrap-ups and the Vocabulary Self-Tests, and all five will help learners make steady progress in developing their reading, vocabulary, and other English language skills.

Linda Butler, creator of the Password *series*

Additional References

Nation, Paul. *Teaching and Learning Vocabulary.* New York: Newbury House, 1990.

Schmitt, Norbert, and Michael McCarthy, eds. *Vocabulary: Description, Acquisition, and Pedagogy.* Cambridge, UK: Cambridge University Press, 1997.

Schmitt, Norbert, and Cheryl Boyd Zimmerman. "Derivative Word Forms: What Do Learners Know?" *TESOL Quarterly* 36 (Summer 2002): 145–171.

---

[4]Dilin Liu, "The Most Frequently Used Spoken American English Idioms: A Corpus Analysis and Its Implications," *TESOL Quarterly* 37 (Winter 2003): 671–700.
[5]Nation, 254.

OVERVIEW OF *NEW PASSWORD 4*

New Password 4 is intended for students with a vocabulary of about 1,200 words in English, and it teaches over 300 more. Fifteen words and phrases from each nonfiction reading passage are targeted in the exercises for that chapter and recycled in later chapters. Because of the systematic building of vocabulary, as well as the progression of reading skills work, it is best to do the chapters in order.

Most of the target words are among the 1,500 highest-frequency words in English, words that students need to build a solid foundation for their language learning. Other, lower-frequency words and phrases are targeted for their usefulness in discussing a particular theme, such as *carbon dioxide, resource,* and *renewable* in Unit 4: The Environment.

Organization of the Book

New Password 4 contains five units, each with four chapters followed by a Wrap-up section. Vocabulary Self-Tests are found after Units 2, 4, and 5. At the end of the book you will find the Vocabulary Self-Tests Answer Key and an index to the target vocabulary.

THE UNITS

Each unit is based on a theme and includes four chapters, each of which is built around a nonfiction reading passage.

THE CHAPTERS

Each chapter is organized as follows:

Getting Ready to Read—The chapter opens with a photo and prereading tasks. Some tasks are for pair or small-group work, others for the full class. *Getting Ready to Read* starts students thinking about the subject of the reading by drawing on what they know, eliciting their opinions, and introducing relevant vocabulary.

Reading—The reading passages progress from about 600 to about 750 words over the course of the book, and they increase in level of reading difficulty. Students should read each passage the first time without stopping to look up or ask about new words. Let them know that the goal for this first reading is to get the main ideas and that multiple readings are essential to improve their comprehension and reading fluency. You may wish to have them reread while you read aloud or play the audio, as listening while reading can aid comprehension, retention, and pronunciation. The reading is followed by *Quick Comprehension Check,* a brief true/false exercise to let students check their general understanding. It is a good idea to go over the *Quick Comprehension Check* statements in class: When a statement is true, ask students how they know it is true; when it is false, have students correct it. By doing so, you send them back into the reading to find support for their answers. Try to avoid spending time explaining vocabulary at this point.

Exploring Vocabulary—Once students have a general understanding of the reading, it is time to focus on new words. This section has two parts:

1. *Thinking about the Target Vocabulary.* In Chapter 1, students see the target words and phrases from the reading passage listed in a chart under *Nouns, Verbs, Adjectives,* and *Other.** From Chapter 2 on, students are asked to find target words and phrases in the reading and write them in the correct column of the chart. Students then identify the vocabulary that is new to them and return to the reading to see what they can learn about word meanings from context. (See the Scope and Sequence on pages iv–vii for chapter-by-chapter lists of the target vocabulary and the index on page 267 for an alphabetized list.)

2. *Using the Target Vocabulary.* This section has two exercises to help students understand the meanings of the target vocabulary as used in the reading. The exercises can be done in class or out, by students working individually or in pairs.

Developing Reading Skills—In this section are tasks that require students to delve back into the reading. They include work on understanding main ideas, major points, and supporting details, distinguishing fact from opinion, understanding reference words, making inferences and comparisons, assessing the writer's purpose and point of view, quoting, paraphrasing, and summarizing. The exercises reflect the range of skills that students must develop for academic reading and require students to interact with the texts in a variety of ways. As students often vary widely in the time they need to complete such work, it may be best done outside of class.

---

* In the chart, *Nouns* include noun phrases (such as *the economy*), *Verbs* include phrasal verbs (such as *come up with* and *set up*) and verb phrases (such as *make a living* and *have something to do with*), *Adjectives* include participial adjectives (such as *confused* and *developing*), and *Other* includes adverbs, prepositions, etc.

Expanding Vocabulary—This section has three parts:

1. *New Contexts*. Two exercises recycle the target vocabulary and let students see it used in contexts unrelated to the reading.
2. *Building on the Vocabulary*. Here you will find either *Word Grammar*, with work on parts of speech or the meanings and uses of particular target words, or *Studying Collocations*, with information on words that go together, such as combinations of noun/verb/adjective + preposition, or nouns that pair up with certain verbs. (See the Scope and Sequence on pages iv–vii for the contents of *Building on the Vocabulary* sections.)
3. *Using New Words*. Here is a chance for students to work productively with the target vocabulary, creating sentences of their own, either in class with a partner or working alone. Encourage students to experiment with the words and phrases they understand least.

Putting It All Together—This section begins with *Discussion, Sharing Opinions,* or *Role-play,* which require critical thinking about the reading and combine it with fluency-building work. The questions are not intended to test students' recall but rather to deepen their understanding of the material, so students should be able to refer back to the reading as needed. The chapter ends with *Writing,* which offers a choice of paragraph-writing assignments. These may be used for brief in-class writing, as prompts for journal entries, or for more formal and extended assignments.

UNIT WRAP-UP

Each unit ends with a Wrap-up section that gives students a key follow-up to their initial encounters with the unit vocabulary, to consolidate and enrich their understanding of new words and phrases and to broaden their understanding of word families and dictionary use. It has four parts: *Reviewing Vocabulary, Expanding Vocabulary, A Puzzle,* and *Building Dictionary Skills,* which features excerpts from the fourth edition of the *Longman Dictionary of American English.*

The Teacher's Manual

The Teacher's Manual for *New Password 4* contains:

- The answer key for all exercises in the book
- Five unit tests with answers
- Quick Oral Reviews, sets of prompts you can use for rapid drills of vocabulary studied in each chapter. These drills can be an important part of the spaced repetition of vocabulary—repeated exposures to newly learned words and phrases at increasing intervals—that helps students remember the vocabulary. For tips on how to use the prompts, see the Introduction in the Teacher's Manual.

To the Student

Welcome to *New Password 4*! This book will help you improve your reading skills in English and expand your English vocabulary. I hope you will enjoy reading, writing, and talking about the people, events, and ideas described in the text.

About the Author

Linda Butler began her English-language teaching career in Italy in 1979. She currently teaches ESL part-time at Holyoke Community College in Holyoke, Massachusetts. She is the author of many ESL/EFL textbooks, including Books 1 through 4 of the *New Password* series and *Fundamentals of Academic Writing.*

REFERENCES, ACKNOWLEDGMENTS, AND CREDITS

REFERENCES

Barasch, D. "Letter from the Editor: Why I Ain't Blue." *OnEarth Magazine,* Vol. 28, No. 2, Summer 2006, p. 3.

Field, L. "Young entrepreneur turns hobby into career." *Opelika-Auburn News,* September 29, 2007: NA.

Leonhardt, D. "Maybe Money Does Buy Happiness After All." *New York Times,* April 16, 2008 [electronic version].

Levy, S. "The Vanishing." *OnEarth Magazine,* Vol. 28, No. 2, Summer 2006, pp. 14–22.

Nadkarni, N. M. *Between Earth and Sky: Our intimate connections to trees.* Berkeley, CA: University of California Press, 2008.

Tozzi, J. "Should You Hire Your Parents?" *Business Week.* Retrieved January 12, 2009, from http://images.businessweek.com/ss/08/09/0908_2008_entrepreneurs/6.htm.

Silverman, G. "Book Summary: *Secrets of Word of Mouth Marketing.*" Retrieved January 12, 2009, from http://www.bizsum.com/articles/art_the-secrets-of-word-of-mouth-marketing.php.

Stevenson, B., and Wolfers, J. "Economic Growth and Subjective Well-Being: Reassessing the Easterlin Paradox." Retrieved January 6, 2009, from http://bpp.wharton.upenn.edu/betseys/papers/happiness.pdf.

"Teen Millionaires . . . How Did They Do It?" *The Morning Show.* Retrieved January 12, 2009, from http://www.youtube.com/watch?v=MZXHlLQGquQ&feature=related.

ACKNOWLEDGMENTS

For their help with the research for *New Password 4,* I would like to thank Maggie Butler and Stephen Roy; for editorial feedback, Jim Montgomery, Lynn Stafford-Yilmaz, and Jane Sloan; and for research and editorial assistance, Miles Montgomery-Butler. For his sense of humor and his tireless scrutiny of all five *New Password* texts, I am particularly grateful to developmental editor Tom Ormond. I would also like to thank Lynn Bonesteel, author of *New Password 5,* and Helen Ambrosio, Project Editor, for their contributions to the series.

I also very much appreciate the work of the following reviewers, who commented on early drafts of materials for the book: Simon Weedon, NOVA ICI Oita School, Japan; Joe Walther, Sookmyung Women's University, Korea; Kevin Knight, Kanda University of International Studies, Japan; Guy Elders, Turkey; Wendy Allison, Seminole Community College, Florida; Kimberly Bayer-Olthoff, Hunter College, New York; Ruth Ann Weinstein, J. E. Burke High School, Massachusetts; Vincent LoSchiavo, P.S. 163, New York; Kelly Roberts-Weibel, Edmunds Community College, Washington; Lisa Cook, Laney College, California; Thomas Leverett, Southern Illinois University, Illinois; Angela Parrino, Hunter College, New York; Adele Camus, George Mason University, Virginia.

Finally, it has been a pleasure working with Pearson Longman ELT, and for all their efforts on behalf of this book and the entire *New Password* series, I would like to thank Pietro Alongi, Editorial Director; Amy McCormick, Acquisitions Editor; Paula Van Ells, Director of Development; Thomas Ormond, Development Editor; Susan Tait Porcaro and Wendy Duran, Illustrators; Wendy Campbell and Carlos Rountree, Assistant Editors and the rest of the Pearson Longman ELT team.

TEXT CREDITS

p. 15, Adapted from "Word-of-mouth Marketing" by Dan Forbush, *Scope Quarterly,* Fall 2008. Used with permission of the author; p. 161, Adapted from "Two Strokes and You're Out" by David Kushner, *Discovery Magazine,* published online May 21, 2008. Used with permission of the author; p. 182, Adapted from "Want to Help the Environment? Eat Insects." by Josie Glausiusz, *Discover Magazine,* published online May 7, 2008. Used with permission.

PHOTOGRAPHY CREDITS

p. 1, © *Herrmann/Starke/Corbis;* p. 2, © *Can Stock Photo;* p. 14, © *Fancy/Veer/CORBIS;* p. 25, © *Arlene Jean Gee/shutterstock;* p. 36, © *Andrew Holbrooke;* p. 53, © *EastWest Imaging/fotolia;* page 54, © *absolut/shutterstock;* p. 64, © *Zsolt Nyulaszi/shutterstock;* p. 77, © *Serge Kozak/Corbis;* p. 88, © *Thomas Roepke/Corbis;* p. 108, © *1999 by Geoffrey Wheeler;* p. 119, © *Andrey Fomenko. Image from BigStockPhoto.com;* p. 141, © *Forrest J. Ackerman Collection/Corbis;* p. 159, © *drserg/shutterstock;* p. 160, © *Mayangsari/Dreamstime.com;* p. 171, by Clare Montgomery-Butler; p. 181, © *frans lemmens/Alamy;* p. 192, © *shutterstock;* p. 211, © *Chepko Danil Vitalevich/shutterstock;* p. 212 © *istockphoto;* p. 222, © *Randy Faris/Corbis;* p. 246, © *Vanderbilt University*

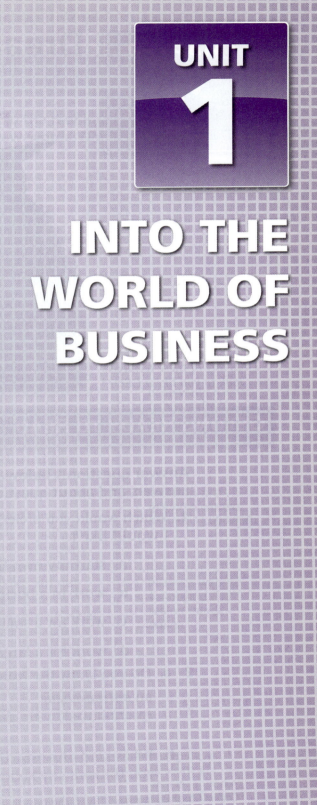

UNIT
1

INTO THE WORLD OF BUSINESS

5   Young people who start their own businesses may face problems that older people do not. Matt Spain is one example. He started a computer **service** company at age fifteen. That was old enough to be good at fixing computers, but not old enough to drive. His **clients** had to pick him up and take him to work on their computers.

6   Young CEOs may also face a question that older ones do not: Should they hire their parents? Ashley Qualls hired her mother. Daniel Negari did, too. He started working in real estate[5] at age eighteen, and at twenty-two, he had fourteen people working for him. He got his mother to leave her high-paying job to work for him by showing her that with his company, she would earn even more. He was happy to hire someone he knew so well and trusted completely.

[5] *real estate = the business of selling houses, other buildings, or land*

7   Young or old, most entrepreneurs are alike in some ways. For example, they are **willing** to take **risks**, and they believe they will succeed. If you would like to know more about starting your own business, you can pick up a book about it. Cameron Johnson wrote his first at age fifteen.

Quick Comprehension Check

Read these sentences. Circle T (true) or F (false).

1. Entrepreneurs are people who start their own businesses. (T) F

2. Some famous businesses have been started by college students.   T   F

3. Young entrepreneurs get good experience but little money.   T   F

4. The young people in the reading all had the goal of getting rich.   T   F

5. Young CEOs and older ones share all the same problems. T   F

6. Starting your own business means taking chances.   T   F

EXPLORING VOCABULARY

Thinking about the Target Vocabulary

 A The words and phrases in **bold** in "Dreamers and Doers" are the **target vocabulary** for this chapter. They are listed in this chart in the same order as in the reading. Notice that:

- In the column on the left are the paragraph numbers.
- The next three columns are for nouns, verbs, and adjectives—three important **parts of speech**. The last column is for all other kinds of words and phrases.

	Nouns*	Verbs*	Adjectives	Other
1		come up with		
		turn something into		
2		set up		
	ad			
		earn		
3		drive		
		mean		
4		make a living		
		hire		
			fair	
		design		
5	service			
	client			
7			willing	
	risk			

*The chart shows the singular form of any plural noun from the reading. It shows the base form, or simple form, of each verb. "Verbs" include phrasal verbs, such as *come up with* (see page 11 for more information), and verb phrases, such as *make a living*.

B Which words or phrases are new to you? Circle them here. Then find them in the reading. Look at the context. Can you guess the meaning?

Guessing Meaning from Context

We use words in a **context**. The context of a word means the words and sentences before and after the word. The context can help you guess the meaning of a word or phrase. For example, look at the context of *make a living*:

> [Constanza] met some people who were highly skilled at making clothes but could not **make a living** at it. Instead, they supported themselves washing dishes or cleaning rooms.

The context of *make a living* tells you that the phrase refers to work. The people could not make a living at one thing, so they did other work. They did it to support themselves. The context tells you that *make a living* means to make enough money from your work to support yourself.

Using the Target Vocabulary

A These sentences are **about the reading**. Complete them with the words and phrases in the box.

✓ came up with	drives	fair	service	turned it into
designs	earned	hired	set up	willing

1. If someone was the first person to think of an idea or a plan, for a business or anything else, you can say that he or she ___came up with___ the idea.

2. If someone takes an idea and does the work to change it into something else—a business, for example—you can say the person took the idea and _____ a business.

3. Ashley Qualls learned how to create a website. She learned the steps to make it happen, and then she _____ a website of her own.

4. Ashley made a lot of money from her website while still in high school. She _____ enough money to buy a house.

5. Young entrepreneurs have to do a lot of work to make a business succeed. Something strongly influences them to work so hard. What _____ them to do it?

6. Constanza Ontaneda gave jobs to people who were highly skilled at making clothes. She _____ them to work for her.

7. Some workers do not get paid as much as they should. Constanza wanted to pay her workers the right amount. She hired them at a _____ rate of pay.

8. Constanza comes up with new ideas for clothes and draws pictures of them. She _____ clothes.

9. Matt Spain started a business fixing computers for people. He did not sell a product, as many businesses do. He offered people a _____—a kind of help.

10. Some people don't want to take chances. The idea makes them unhappy. But entrepreneurs are usually ready and _____ to take risks.

B **Read each definition and look at the paragraph number. Look back at the reading on pages 3–4 to find the boldfaced word or phrase to match the definition. Write it in the chart.**

Definition	Paragraph	Target Word or Phrase
1. pictures, words, short movies, etc., used to get people to buy a product, use a service, etc. (short for *advertisements*)	2	*ads*
2. plan (to do something), have something in mind as a purpose	3	
3. earn enough money to live	4	
4. people who pay for services or advice from a professional, a company, etc.	5	
5. chances that bad things may happen	7	

DEVELOPING READING SKILLS

Understanding Topics and Main Ideas

Read about topics and main ideas. Answer the questions.

Every reading is about someone or something. That person or thing is the **topic** of the reading. The title of a reading may tell you what the topic is. The topic can usually be expressed in a word or a phrase.

1. What is the topic of the reading "Dreamers and Doers"? Check (✓) your answer.
   - [ ] **a.** Dreams about the future
   - [ ] **b.** People who start up businesses
   - [ ] **c.** Ways you can make a lot of money

The **main idea** of a reading is the most important information about the topic. Use a complete sentence to express the main idea of a reading.

2. What is the main idea of the reading? Check (✓) your answer.
   - [ ] **a.** It is important for a young person to have a dream about the future.
   - [ ] **b.** Some very young people have become successful entrepreneurs.
   - [ ] **c.** It is easier to start your own business when you are very young.
3. What is the main idea of paragraph 3?
   - [ ] **a.** Young entrepreneurs have various reasons for what they do.
   - [ ] **b.** Most young entrepreneurs start their businesses by accident.
   - [ ] **c.** The dream of becoming a CEO drives the average entrepreneur.
4. What is the main idea of paragraph 6? Write a sentence.

_____

Reading for Details

Are these statements about the reading true or false? If the reading doesn't give the information, check (✔) *It doesn't say*.

	True	False	It doesn't say
1. Facebook and Microsoft are examples of businesses begun by college students.	☑	☐	☐
2. Ashley Qualls set up her website to make money.	☐	☐	☐
3. Cameron Johnson made a lot of money as a young entrepreneur.	☐	☐	☐
4. Pierre Omidyar set up his business and then sold it.	☐	☐	☐
5. The people who work for Constanza Ontaneda get a fair paycheck.	☐	☐	☐
6. Ontaneda hired her mother to work for her.	☐	☐	☐
7. Daniel Negari has a computer service company.	☐	☐	☐
8. Entrepreneurs of any age must be willing to take risks.	☐	☐	☐

EXPANDING VOCABULARY

New Contexts

A **Complete the sentences with the target words and phrases in the box. There are two extra words.**

ads	design	fair	mean	services
clients	drive	✓make a living	risks	willing

1. Jack takes beautiful photos, but he can't ___make a living___ at it.
2. An architect is a person whose job is to _____ houses and other buildings.

3. A doctor has patients, a store owner has customers, and a lawyer has

_____.

4. Commercials are _____ that we see on TV or hear on the radio.

5. Tony understands the _____, but he wants to be a racecar driver anyway.

6. The company offers nighttime cleaning _____ for office buildings.

7. Jan was angry that Peter wasn't doing his _____ share of the work.

8. I'm sorry about what I said. I didn't _____ to upset you.

B   These sentences also use the target words and phrases **in new contexts. What is the meaning of each boldfaced word or phrase? Circle a, b, or c.**

1. *Minimum wage* means the lowest hourly rate that someone can **earn** by law. *Earn* means

   a. pay as a tax.   **b.** get by working.   **c.** save in the bank.

2. Higher oil prices are **driving** price increases for everything else. In this sentence, *driving* means

   a. allowing.   **b.** holding back.   **c.** causing.

3. I have no idea yet what to get him as a gift, but I'll **come up with** something. *Come up with* means

   a. arrive with.   **b.** think of.   **c.** bring.

4. Business is slow, so no one is **hiring**. *Hiring* means

   a. giving jobs to   **b.** making a lot   **c.** working long hours.
   new workers.   of money.

5. Chris has taken a bedroom and **turned it into** a home office. *Turn something into* means

   a. call it.   **b.** change it into.   **c.** imagine it as.

6. Nick and his friends are **setting up** a new after-school club. *Set something up* means
   a. start it.   **b.** ask for it.   **c.** join it.

7. I like the car, but I'm not **willing** to pay that price for it. *Willing to do something* means
   a. knowing how to do it.   **b.** ready and often happy to do it.   **c.** too afraid to do it.

Building on the Vocabulary: Word Grammar

The **parts of speech** are the different kinds of words. Understanding the parts of speech will help you understand how to use words in sentences.

The parts of speech include:

Nouns: These are words for people (*boy, clients, Ashley*), things (*book, ads, Honda*), places (*home, airport, Los Angeles*), and ideas (*risks, education, time*).

Verbs: Every sentence must have a verb. Verbs are words for actions (*dance, go, run, wash*) or for states or experiences (*be, have, feel, understand*). **Phrasal verbs** combine a verb with a particle, as in *set up* and *turn into*. The meaning of a phrasal verb can be very different from the meaning of the verb alone.

Read the sentences. Underline the verbs. Circle the nouns.

1. Who came up with the idea for the movie?
2. Most entrepreneurs take risks.
3. The company hired Paula right after her interview.
4. I'm planning to take a trip to New York City.
5. The magazine had many pages full of ads.
6. Pam didn't know how difficult the job was going to be.
7. Ashley learned how to set up a website.
8. I'm sure the boys didn't mean to break the window.

Using New Words

Work with a partner. Choose five of the target words or phrases from the chart on page 5. On a piece of paper, use each word or phrase in a sentence. Do not choose the ones that you can use easily. This is a chance to learn more about words or phrases that you do not understand well.

Examples:

My friend's father helped me get a job by <u>setting up</u> an interview for me at his company.

I am <u>willing</u> to work very hard to learn English.

PUTTING IT ALL TOGETHER

Discussion

Talk with a partner or in a small group about the questions below.

1. The reading describes six young entrepreneurs. What facts do you remember about each one? Whose story is most interesting to you? Explain why.

2. Compare young entrepreneurs with older ones. How are they alike, and how are they different? Use information from the reading, and add your own ideas.

3. What do you think the title "Dreamers and Doers" means? Why do you think the writer chose this as the title for the reading?

Writing

Choose a topic. Write a paragraph.

1. Choose a young entrepreneur from "Dreamers and Doers" whom you find interesting. Tell what you know about this person and what you think about his or her story.

2. Look back at question 1 on page 2. What was your first choice? Explain why you would prefer that to the other choices.

Example:

One of the interesting young entrepreneurs described in "Dreamers and Doers" is Matt Spain. He started his own business, a computer service company, when he was only fifteen years old. He knew how to fix computers, but he did not know how to drive, so he had to ask his clients for rides. I wonder if that was embarrassing for him. Maybe it made his clients think about how young he was and wonder if he was old enough to trust with their computers. I think it probably was not a problem because I know adults who depend on teenagers for help with their computers.

CHAPTER 2

Word-of-Mouth Advertising

"Try it. You'll like it."

GETTING READY TO READ

Talk about these questions with a partner and then with your class.

1. Where do you see ads? On a piece of paper, make a list of all the places you can think of.

2. How do you feel about the ads you see and hear? Check (✓) one or more answers.

   ☐ Ads are a good way to learn about products.

   ☐ Ads are often interesting and fun.

   ☐ I don't usually pay much attention to ads.

   ☐ I hate ads.

Look at the pictures, words, and definitions next to the reading. Then read without stopping. Don't worry about new words. Don't stop to use a dictionary. Just keep reading!

Word-of-Mouth Advertising

1   Whether you want to or not, you probably see and hear ads every day. Ads are all around us and have been for a very long time. They have even been found painted on walls in the ruins[1] of Pompeii and ancient[2] Egypt. **Advertising** has come a long way[3] since then, but it is still all about getting people's attention.

2   Back when few people could read, ads usually took the form of pictures. A sign for a shoemaker might have a picture of a boot, and a sign for a baker might show a loaf of bread. Street callers were a common form of advertising, too. They were hired to **announce** in a loud voice what was for sale, where to find it, and how good it was, as in "Get your fresh fish, right here, right now! The best in town!"

3   In **developing** countries, some businesses still use street callers, and this form of advertising probably does not cost them very much. In other parts of the world, advertising has become much more sophisticated,[4] and it costs a great deal. If you add up all the money spent on advertising around the world, it comes to the equivalent of[5] hundreds of billions[6] of U.S. dollars a year.

4   Business owners will consider it money well spent **as long as** enough **consumers** pay attention and buy the product or use the service. But much of the time, consumers do not pay attention. When an ad comes on the TV or radio, they change the station. They turn the pages of magazines without really seeing the ads. If an ad **appears** on their computer **screen**, they **get rid of** it or just look away.

5   Dave Balter worked in advertising, and he knew that most people do not like ads. They **avoid** watching them, reading them, or listening to them. He also knew that people do pay attention when they hear about **goods** and services from people they know. So he said to himself, "If no one pays attention to advertising, but

(continued)

[1] *ruins*

[2] *ancient* = happening or existing very far back in history

[3] *has come a long way* = has changed a lot (for the better)

[4] *sophisticated* = having a complex and advanced design

[5] *the equivalent of* = an amount that is the same as

[6] a *billion* = 1,000,000,000

they do pay attention to the opinions of their friends and family, let's focus our attention there. Let's figure out a better way."

6   What Balter came up with was a website where consumers could **sign up** to receive free products. **In return**, they promised that if they liked the products, they would tell their friends. In most cases, the **volunteers** also got coupons[7] to give to their friends. All Balter asked was that they report back on two questions: What did you think of the product, and who did you talk to about it? Balter then reported back to his clients, the companies who had hired him.

7   After four years, Balter had 65,000 volunteers trying products and telling people about the ones they liked. Then a reporter heard about Balter's idea and wrote a story on it for a **major** magazine. Free advertising! Within a year after that story appeared, Balter had 130,000 volunteers. Today, he has over 400,000. Balter has advertised a wide variety of products with the help of these volunteers. They are doing word-of-mouth advertising, perhaps the best kind there is.

8   There may be a risk to advertising by word of mouth, however, according to George Silverman, author of *The Secrets of Word-of-Mouth Marketing*. What is the danger? Studies have shown that a customer who likes a product or service will tell an average of three people about it. But when she does not like one, she will tell eleven. This means that **while** good word of mouth can help, bad word of mouth can really hurt.

[7] *a coupon*

Quick Comprehension Check

Read these sentences. Circle T (true) or F (false).

1. Advertising is a modern invention.   T   F

2. Some forms of advertising are low cost.   T   F

3. Billions of dollars are spent on ads each year.   T   F

4. Dave Balter believes most people enjoy ads.   T   F

5. People usually listen to their friends' opinions
    of products.   T   F

6. Dave Balter pays people to try new products.   T   F

EXPLORING VOCABULARY

Thinking about the Target Vocabulary

 Find the five verbs in **bold** in "Word-of-Mouth Advertising." Add them to the chart. Write them in the order they appear in the reading. Use the base form of each verb.

	Nouns	Verbs	Adjectives	Other
1	advertising			
2				
3			developing	
4				as long as
	consumer			
	screen			
5				
	goods*			
6				
				in return
	volunteer			
7			major	
8				while

* Use this noun in the plural only.

B Which words or phrases are new to you? Circle them here. Then find them in the reading. Look at the context. Can you guess the meaning?

Using the Target Vocabulary

 These sentences are **about the reading**. Complete them with the words and phrases in the box.

advertising	as long as	in return	sign up
appears	avoid	screen	while

1. The business of creating and using ads is called _____.

2. Business owners are willing to spend money on advertising if the ads get them customers. They don't mind spending the money _____ the ads work.

3. Sometimes you suddenly see an ad on your computer. The ad _____ on your computer.

4. The part of your computer where ads appear, or where you see a video or words, is called the _____.

5. Many people try not to watch, read, or listen to ads. They _____ ads.

6. Dave Balter set up a website where a person could put his or her name on a list to get free products. A person could _____ to get the products.

7. The people who got the free products promised to do something as a kind of payment. They promised to do something _____.

8. Although word-of-mouth advertising can have a good effect, it can also have a very bad one. _____ good word of mouth is helpful, bad word of mouth can really hurt. (In this case, *while* does not refer to time; it shows a difference between two things.)

B These sentences are also about the reading. What is the meaning of each **boldfaced** word or phrase? Circle a, b, or c.

1. The job of a street caller was to **announce** what was for sale. *Announce* means
   a. make a decision.
   b. give out new information.
   c. set something up.

2. In **developing** countries, most businesses cannot afford expensive advertising. A developing nation is
   a. poor but trying to produce more.
   b. full of successful businesses.
   c. not willing to do business.

3. Advertisers want **consumers** to pay attention to ads. Consumers are people who
   a. work for a living.
   b. buy products and services.
   c. own personal computers.

4. If an ad appears on your computer screen, you may want to **get rid of** it. *Get rid of something* means to take action so that you
   a. don't have it anymore.
   b. can pay for it later.
   c. put it in a safe place.

5. We usually pay attention to our friends' opinions of **goods** and services. *Goods* means
   a. products.
   b. nice people.
   c. interesting places.

6. Dave Balter got **volunteers** to do word-of-mouth advertising for his clients. Volunteers are people who
   a. like to take risks.
   b. work without pay.
   c. earn a lot of money.

7. A story in a **major** magazine brought Balter a lot of attention. In this sentence, *major* means
   a. small.
   b. fair.
   c. important.

DEVELOPING READING SKILLS

Scanning

Scan the reading on pages 15–16 for the information to complete these sentences. Where you see quotation marks (" "), be sure to copy the exact words from the reading.

1. Advertising is "all about _____."

2. Before most people could read, business owners often used

   _____ and _____.

3. Worldwide, advertising costs _____ a year.

4. Dave Balter knew that consumers pay attention to what _____

   _____ say about _____.

5. Balter's idea was to get volunteers to do _____

   advertising.

6. In the opinion of George Silverman, "there _____

   _____."

7. Studies show that a customer will, on average:

   a. tell _____ people about a product or service that she likes.

   b. tell _____ people about one that she doesn't like.

Understanding Topics and Main Ideas

 Where in the reading can you find these topics? Write the paragraph number.

_3_ **a.** advertising costs

____ **b.** a risk of word-of-mouth advertising

____ **c.** two early forms of advertising

____ **d.** what consumers often do about ads

_____ **e.** the early history and main purpose of advertising

_____ **f.** Balter's plan

_____ **g.** the success of Balter's plan

_____ **h.** Balter's ideas about consumers and ads

B **Complete the sentence to give the main idea of the paragraph. Do not copy sentences from the reading. Use your own words.**

1. Paragraph 3: Advertising may be simple and cheap in developing countries, but _____

_____.

2. Paragraph 4: Business owners are willing to pay for ads if consumers pay attention to them, but _____

_____.

EXPANDING VOCABULARY

New Contexts

A **Complete the sentences with the target words and phrases in the box. There are two extra words or phrases.**

advertising	avoiding	goods	major
announced	consumers	got rid of	volunteers
as long as	developing	in return	while

1. The company president _____ the hiring of 1,000 new workers.

2. When we bought our new TV, we _____ our old one.

3. _____ the job would be interesting, the pay would be low.

4. All the _____ TV news programs sent reporters to cover the story.

5. The schools need _____ to help teachers in grades one through five.

6. U.S. _____ spend a lot of money Christmas shopping in December.

7. George smiled at Carmen, and she smiled _____.

8. The police say they found stolen _____ in the apartment.

9. The World Bank means to do more to help _____ nations in Africa.

10. This cereal costs more than that one only because the first company spends more on _____.

 Read these sentences. Write the boldfaced target words or phrases next to their definitions. There is one extra definition. Put an X next to it.

a. My new computer has a 15-inch **screen**.

b. Nancy's cat was lost for days but then **appeared** at her door.

c. I try to **avoid** having to stand in lines.

d. Are you going to **sign up** to take the class?

e. Lisa's father said she could go out **as long as** she did her homework first.

Target Words or Phrases	Definitions
1. _____	= if
2. _____	= enjoy, have fun doing
3. _____	= started to be seen or was suddenly seen
4. _____	= put your name on a list because you want to join
5. _____	= do something to stop something bad from happening
6. _____	= the flat part of a TV or computer where you see words, pictures, etc.

Building on the Vocabulary: Word Grammar

> In addition to nouns and verbs, **adjectives** are one of the major parts of speech. Adjectives, such as *happy*, *hot*, *rich*, and *new*, describe people, places, things, and ideas. Adjectives come before nouns (*an* **old** *man, an* **interesting** *book*) or after linking verbs such as *be*, *seem*, and *look* (*I'm* **ready**. *It* **seems** **expensive**. *You* **look** **tired**.)
>
> Most adjectives have a **comparative** form (*a* **lighter** *color, a* **more difficult** *test*) and a **superlative** form (*the* **fastest** *runner in the world,* *the* **worst** *storm of the year*).

Circle the adjectives in these sentences.

1. It was a (common) form of advertising.
2. The game was exciting.
3. She designs beautiful buildings.
4. We agreed that it was fair.
5. He's taller than I am.
6. He said, "Let's figure out a better way."
7. I'm willing to try if you are.
8. Major stories appear on page one of the newspaper.

Using New Words

Work with a partner. Choose five of the target words or phrases from the chart on page 17. On a piece of paper, use each word or phrase in a sentence. Remember: Do not choose the ones that you can use easily. This is a chance to learn more about words or phrases that you do not understand well.

Examples:

While it is very useful to have a car, it is also very expensive.

When someone says, "Hello" to me, I say, "Hello" in return.

PUTTING IT ALL TOGETHER

Discussion

Talk with a small group about the questions below.

1. The reading describes Dave Balter's idea for using volunteers to advertise his clients' products. What does a volunteer have to do? Complete this list of the steps:

   1. Go to Balter's website.

   2. . . .

2. Describe an ad that you remember seeing. What made the ad easy to remember? Do you remember what product or service it advertised? Did you buy the product or use the service because of the ad?

3. Why can word-of-mouth advertising be good for a business compared to other types of advertising? When would other kinds of advertising be better? Consider the type of product or service being advertised, the market for it, the question of time, and so on.

Writing

Choose a topic. Write a paragraph.

1. Write instructions for someone who wants to be a volunteer for Dave Balter. If you wish, you can begin:

   According to "Word-of-Mouth Advertising," if you want to be a volunteer for Dave Balter, you have to do several things. First, . . .

2. Look back at question 2 on page 14. Use one of the statements as the first sentence in a paragraph. Then explain your feelings about ads.

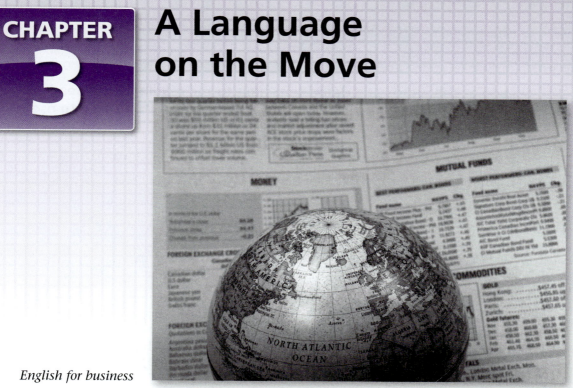

CHAPTER 3

A Language on the Move

English for business

GETTING READY TO READ

Answer parts a, b, and c of question 1 by circling a number from 1 to 5. Then talk about your answers to questions 1 and 2 in a small group or with your class.

Very ←——————→ Not at all

1. In your country:

   a. Are English classes common in
      the schools?   1   2   3   4   5

   b. Is English important for many jobs?   1   2   3   4   5

   c. Is English important in the
      business world?   1   2   3   4   5

2. When, where, and why do people from your country use English to do business?

READING

Look at the words and definitions next to the reading. Then read without stopping. Don't worry about new words. Don't stop to use a dictionary. Just keep reading!

A Language on the Move

1   Filiz Yilmaz works for a company in Istanbul and usually speaks Turkish at work. When she travels to England on business, she uses English. But when she goes to Germany or Brazil, she does not use German or Portuguese. She **deals with** people there in English. "I use English in Japan and Thailand, too," she says. "It's the language of international business."

2   How did English get to be so popular? It is not the oldest living language or the most beautiful to the ear. It has sounds that are hard to pronounce and words that are hard to spell. So why has this **particular** language **spread** so far?

3   Some people would answer by pointing to the influence of movies and music. However, films made in English often appear in other languages, and people can enjoy songs in English without understanding the words. So this does not tell the whole story.[1]

4   Part of the answer can be found in the **nature** of the language. English has certain **qualities** that make it especially useful. For one thing, its grammar is **quite** simple. For example, learners of English do not have to worry about whether a noun is masculine, feminine, or neuter,[2] while learners of many other languages do. In German, for example, *der Mond* (the word for the moon) is masculine but *die Sonne* (the sun) is feminine. Anyone would expect the words for girl and woman (*das Mädchen* and *das Weib*) to be feminine, but they are neuter!

5   English also has a **huge** vocabulary. Early English developed from Germanic languages, which gave it its most common words, such as *the, is, of, go, you, man,* and *woman.* English has always taken words from other European languages, too, including Latin (*attract, design,* and *invent*) and Greek (*alphabet, mathematics,* and *theater*). After 1066, when invaders[3] from France **took over**, English **gained** many French words, such as *officer, crime,* and *service.* Since that time, English has welcomed words from many other languages— Spanish, Arabic, Turkish, Urdu, Chinese, and Japanese, to name just a few.

[1] *tell the whole story* = explain everything

[2] *masculine, feminine, or neuter* = male, female, or neither

[3] *invaders* = people who enter a country by force, as with an army

6 To understand the spread of English, we also have to look at **political** and **economic** history. During the 1600s and 1700s, people from England traveled all over the world, taking their language to North America, Africa, India, and Australia. New nations were born, and their governments used English. Then in the 1800s, England led the Industrial Revolution,[4] and London became the world's great financial[5] center. That made English the language of money. In the 1900s, it also became the language of science and air travel.

7 Then came the Internet. As Filiz Yilmaz remembers it, "People at my company realized that the Internet could be quite useful to us. But at first, everything online was in English. It gave us another reason to know this language." Soon businesspeople in many countries were going online and using English more and more.

8 Today, there are business schools teaching all their courses in English even in countries where English is a foreign language. These schools want their students to be ready to **trade** in international **markets**. Companies around the world are **investing** in English classes for their **employees**. They see English as the language of the future.

9 There are over 300 million native speakers of English.[6] Many more people speak Mandarin Chinese—almost 900 million—but few of them are outside China. People who speak English live and work all over the world. There may be a billion people who speak it as a second, third, or fourth language. Filiz says, "With so many people using English, I can't imagine any other language taking its place. I think English for business is here to stay."

[4] *the Industrial Revolution =* the start of producing many goods in factories with machines

[5] *financial =* relating to money or managing money

[6] *native speakers of English =* people whose first language is English

Quick Comprehension Check

Read these sentences. Circle T (true) or F (false).

1. People around the world use English to talk about business.   T F

2. Hollywood movies are the biggest reason why English is so popular.   T F

3. Many English words come from other languages.   T F

4. England was a world power before the United States.   T F

5. Companies around the world think English is the language of the future.   T F

6. The same numbers of people speak Mandarin and English.   T F

EXPLORING VOCABULARY

Thinking about the Target Vocabulary

 A Find the four nouns and four adjectives in **bold** in "A Language on the Move." Add them to the chart. Write them in the order they appear in the reading. Use the singular form of any plural noun.

	Nouns	Verbs	Adjectives	Other
1		deal with		
2				
		spread		
4				
				quite
5				
		take over		
		gain		
6				
8		trade		
		invest		

 B Which words or phrases are new to you? Circle them here. Then find them in the reading. Look at the context. Can you guess the meaning?

Using the Target Vocabulary

 Complete these sentences **about the reading**. Use the words and phrases in the box.

invests	particular	qualities	spread
markets	political	quite	trade

1. The reading gives some history about one _____ language, English (meaning that certain language and no other).

2. The number of English speakers has grown. The language has _____ around the world.

3. English has certain _____. A particular set of these are what make one person or thing different from others.

4. The grammar of English is _____ simple compared to many other languages. (This means the grammatical rules are not very hard, but not completely simple either.)

5. To understand why English has spread over so much of the world, we have to study _____ history. This is about power, governments, and relationships between countries.

6. It is good for people to be able to do business in more than one language because countries _____ with each other.

7. After finishing business school, some people go on to work in international _____—that is, in areas that deal with buying and selling.

8. When a company _____ in English-language training for its workers, it spends money. It does this because it expects the training to result in more money later.

These sentences are also **about the reading**. What is the meaning of each **boldfaced** word or phrase? Circle a, b, or c.

1. Filiz Yilmaz **deals with** people in several countries. In this sentence, *deals with* means
   a. has trouble with.   **b.** does business with.   **c.** comes up with.

2. One reason for the spread of English is the **nature** of the language. *Nature* means
   a. the spelling rules.   **b.** sounds and music.   **c.** particular qualities.

3. Another important quality of English is its **huge** vocabulary. *Huge* means
   a. very, very big.   **b.** surprising.   **c.** friendly.

4. In 1066, an army from France **took over** in England. *Take over* means
   a. take control.   **b.** take an interest.   **c.** take a long time.

5. English has **gained** many words from other languages. In this sentence, *gain something* means
   a. lose it.   **b.** win it.   **c.** get it.

6. **Economic** history from the 1800s on helps explain the spread of English. *Economic* means relating to
   a. money, goods, and services.   **b.** art, music, and books.   **c.** movies and TV.

7. Many companies have invested in English classes for their **employees**. Their employees are the people who
   a. buy their products.   **b.** work for them.   **c.** volunteer for them.

DEVELOPING READING SKILLS

Reading for Details

Read these sentences. Then reread "A Language on the Move" for the answers. If the reading doesn't give the information, check (✔) *It doesn't say*.

	True	False	It doesn't say
1. Filiz Yilmaz uses English in Japan and Brazil.	☐	☐	☐
2. English grammar has more difficult rules than the grammars of most other languages.	☐	☐	☐
3. English has the largest vocabulary of any language.	☐	☐	☐
4. The Industrial Revolution started in England.	☐	☐	☐
5. English became the language of science in the 1800s.	☐	☐	☐
6. The Internet started in California (USA).	☐	☐	☐
7. Some companies pay for their employees to learn English.	☐	☐	☐
8. More people speak English as their second, third, or fourth language than as their first.	☐	☐	☐

Understanding Topics of Paragraphs

 A **Where is the information about these topics in "A Language on the Move"? Scan the reading and write the paragraph number.**

__6__ **a.** political and economic influences

_____ **b.** numbers of English-speakers

_____ **c.** the effect of the Internet

_____ **d.** Filiz Yilmaz's use of English

_____ **e.** the influence of movies and songs in English

_____ **f.** how English developed its huge vocabulary

_____ **g.** English for international markets

B **On a piece of paper, write a sentence or two about each topic in Part A, beginning with the topic of paragraph 1 and continuing in order. Do not copy sentences from the reading. Use your own words.**

Example:

Paragraph 1: Filiz Yilmaz uses English when she travels to other countries on business.

EXPANDING VOCABULARY

New Contexts

A **Complete the sentences with the target words and phrases in the box. There are two extra words.**

dealt with	employees	huge	particular	qualities
economic	gain	nature	political	take over

1. News about the company always spreads quickly among its

   _____.

2. I've _____ that company for years, but I won't do it

   again. Their customer service has become terrible.

3. What do you hope to _____ from the course?

4. The new CEO will _____ on July 1.

5. It is human _____ to want to feel loved.

6. The phrase _____ *science* refers to the study of government.

7. Our _____ future is looking better: People are getting hired again.

8. Entrepreneurs often take risks. Some risks are small, but some are

_____.

B **Read these sentences. Write the boldfaced target words next to their definitions. There is one extra definition. Put an X next to it.**

a. Are you looking for a **particular** color shirt?

b. Her company has been **quite** successful.

c. Sometimes one country won't **trade** with another for political reasons.

d. When one member of a family gets a cold, it often **spreads** to the rest.

e. They **invested** in oil and ended up getting rich.

f. Ann has all the **qualities** the boss likes: She's smart, hardworking, and creative.

g. The company has customers in Asia, but the main **market** for their software is the United States.

Target Words	Definitions
1. _____	= gave money or bought something in hopes of getting more money later
2. _____	= moves and affects more people or a larger area
3. _____	= parts of someone's nature or character
4. _____	= more than a little but not extremely
5. _____	= stopped something bad from happening
6. _____	= buy and sell goods and services
7. _____	= certain, special (not just any one)
8. _____	= a particular area where a company sells its goods

Building on the Vocabulary: Studying Collocations

Collocations are words that often go together. Some words very often go together, such as *pay + attention* and *worry + about*. Other words never go together. For example, use the verb *do + homework*, never the verb *make + homework*.

Sometimes verbs whose meanings are much the same go with certain nouns only.

- The verb *gain* is often used with the nouns *experience*, *strength*, and *weight*. *Gain* usually means to get more of something over time.
- The verb *earn* can have this same meaning, but *earn* goes with the nouns *money*, *points*, and *a living* (among others).
- *Gain*, *earn*, and *win* can all go with the nouns *love*, *trust*, and *respect*.

Complete the sentences with *earn*, *gain*, or *win*. Use the verb that goes with the noun. There may be more than one possible answer in some cases.

1. The job doesn't pay much, but he'll _____ useful experience.
2. I have to watch what I eat. I _____ weight easily.
3. She was able to _____ the trust of voters.
4. Can you _____ a living working only part-time?
5. The patient is doing exercises to _____ back the strength in his arm.
6. I hope to _____ your respect.

Using New Words

Work with a partner. Choose five of the target words or phrases from the chart on page 28. On a piece of paper, use each word or phrase in a sentence. Remember: Do not choose the ones that you can use easily. This is a chance to learn more about words or phrases that you do not understand well.

Examples:

A new prime minister will <u>take over</u> next week in my country.

I think it is hard to <u>deal with</u> people in English on the phone.

PUTTING IT ALL TOGETHER

Discussion

Work with a partner and take turns asking the questions below.

1. What is Filiz Yilmaz's opinion of English as an international language? Do you agree? Support your opinion with information from the reading or from your own experience.

2. English uses many words taken from other languages. Other languages also have words taken from English. For example, businesspeople in Shanghai might use *boss* and *CEO* even when speaking Chinese. Can you give any examples of:

   • English words that are used in your first language?

   • words from your first language that are used in English?

3. How will knowing English affect your future? How much English do you need to know?

Writing

Choose a topic. Write a paragraph.

1. People invest a lot of time and money in learning English, and nobody wants to waste either one. What three (or more) pieces of advice would you give a new learner on how to invest his or her time and money well? If you wish, you can begin:

   If you want to learn English without wasting time or money, here is my advice.

2. When, where, and why did you start to learn English? How did you feel about that experience?

CHAPTER 4

When the Employees Own the Company

Jeffrey Hamelman, head baker and worker-owner, shows off bread made with King Arthur flour.

GETTING READY TO READ

Talk with a partner or in a small group.

1. Have you ever been the boss at work? Would you like a job where you were the boss? Explain why you would or would not.

2. Who works harder, the owner of a business or the people who work for the business? Tell how you would complete this statement, and explain why:

   When you own a business,

   a. you don't have to work so hard.

   b. you have to work harder.

Look at the picture, words, and definitions next to the reading. Then read without stopping. Don't worry about new words. Don't stop to use a dictionary. Just keep reading!

When the Employees Own the Company

1   King Arthur Flour is the oldest flour company in the United States. Its flour is of very high **quality**. Just ask the people who **bake** with it. All across North America, people who care about making fine bread buy King Arthur flour. The company even has customers in Switzerland, Japan, China, and Saudi Arabia.

2   King Arthur Flour began in 1790 as the Sands, Taylor and Wood Company, and the Sands family has stayed with it all these years. Frank Sands started working there in 1963, when his father was **in charge of** the business, and later his wife, Brinna, joined him there. Frank was the fifth member of the Sands family to lead the company, and the last.

3   When Frank and Brinna decided to retire,[1] none of their children wanted to take over the family business. That meant the future of King Arthur was **uncertain**. Then one evening, Brinna asked Frank, "Who **besides** our kids is most like family?" The answer was clear: The people who worked at the company. Frank and Brinna trusted them to continue the family tradition, so they began to let the employees take over the business. Today, the 160 employees of King Arthur own and run the company.

4   Worker-owned businesses do not all start the same way. In some cases, workers at a successful company find a way to buy it. In other cases, a company fails, but the employees start it up again. Often, a group of people decide to set up a new business together. What makes them want to do this? Some want to be part of the decision making at their workplace. Others want a chance to share in a company's **profits**.

5   There are various types of worker-owned businesses. Some of them make a product, like flour, and others **provide** a service, such as cleaning or health care. There are also various ways to **organize** these businesses. However, most worker-owned businesses share certain important ideas. One idea is that all the workers—not

[1] *retire* = stop working at the end of a career (usually because of old age)

(continued)

just the people in charge—should have the chance to be owners. A second is that all financial[2] information about the company is shared openly with the workers. A third is that the workers should have the **right** to vote on business decisions. Then they have real control. The worker-owners at King Arthur **believe in** these ideas. They are proud to call King Arthur "an employee-owned, open-book, team-managed company."

[2] *financial* = relating to money or managing money

6   Here are the stories of how two more **such** companies began:

7   • Eight employees at a photocopy shop[3] in Massachusetts (USA) were unhappy with their jobs. "Working **conditions** were terrible and the pay was low," says Stephen Roy, one of the eight. "Plus,[4] we had no job **security**—the manager could get rid of any one of us at any time for any reason. We ran the shop for the owners, and we started to ask, 'Why can't we do it for ourselves?'" So they went into business together and started Collective Copies. Twenty-five years later, they have two shops. One afternoon a month, they close their doors to meet and make business decisions.

[3] a *photocopy shop* = a business that uses machines to make copies of print materials

[4] *plus* = and also

8   • In Coamo, Puerto Rico, there were not many jobs for young people. Miriam Rodriguez, who lived in Coamo, wanted to do something about it. She organized a **committee** to work on the problem, and the result of their efforts was a furniture business, Las Flores Metalarte. The business now has more than 150 worker-owners producing tables, chairs, kitchen cabinets,[5] and so on. The success of the company has led to other new businesses in the town, including a sandwich shop and a childcare center.

[5] kitchen *cabinets*

9   According to a study in Italy, worker-owned businesses are good for their **communities**. They lead to a higher quality of life. The researchers who did the study looked at things like health care, education, and social activities in many Italian towns. They also considered problems in the towns, such as crime. They found that towns with more worker-owned businesses were better places to live in almost every way.

Brinna Sands's words come from an article by Per Ola and Emily D'Aulaire, "Baking Up a Business," *Smithsonian* (November 2000): 114–115.

Quick Comprehension Check

Read these sentences. Circle T (true) or F (false).

1. King Arthur Flour was a family business for
   many years.   T   F

2. All worker-owned companies start out as family
   businesses.   T   F

3. The workers at King Arthur bought the company
   after it failed.   T   F

4. Worker-owned businesses are not all the same.   T   F

5. Workers gain more control when they become
   worker-owners.   T   F

6. There are worker-owned businesses only in the
   United States.   T   F

EXPLORING VOCABULARY

Thinking about the Target Vocabulary

 Find the seven nouns and four verbs in bold in "When the Employees Own the Company." Add them to the chart. Write them in the order they appear in the reading. Use the singular form of any plural nouns. Use the base form of each verb.

	Nouns	Verbs	Adjectives	Other
1				
2				in charge of
3			uncertain	
				besides
4				

	Nouns	Verbs	Adjectives	Other
5				
6			such	
7				
8				
9				

 B   Which words and phrases are new to you? Circle them here. Then find them in the reading. Look at the context. Can you guess the meaning?

Using the Target Vocabulary

 A   These sentences are **about the reading**. What is the meaning of each **boldfaced** word or phrase? Circle a, b, or c.

1. Frank Sands was the last of his family to be **in charge of** King Arthur Flour. *In charge of something* means
   a. in need of it.   **b.** happy about it.   **c.** responsible for it.

2. Who would run King Arthur after Frank and Brinna? The company's future was **uncertain**. *Uncertain* means
   a. not willing.   **b.** not clear or decided.   **c.** not surprising.

3. Brinna asked who **besides** their children was most important to them. *Besides* means
   a. because of.   **b.** in addition to.   **c.** in order to.

4. Some workers want to be owners so they can share in the company's **profits**. *Profits* means

   a. money earned from doing business.

   b. decisions to be made.

   c. risks in trying something new.

5. Some businesses produce goods and others **provide** services. *Provide* means

   a. avoid.

   b. waste.

   c. supply.

6. There are various ways to **organize** and run a worker-owned business. *Organize* means

   a. plan or set up.

   b. get rid of.

   c. announce.

7. In a worker-owned business, workers should have the **right** to vote. A right is something that a person

   a. is allowed to do by rule or law.

   b. can never hope to do.

   c. has no choice about.

8. The worker-owners at King Arthur Flour **believe in** certain ideas. *Believe in* means

   a. be sure that something will happen.

   b. feel that something is right and good.

   c. hope that something is true.

9. There are many worker-owned businesses in the world. The reading describes three **such** companies. In this sentence, *such* means

   a. of the kind described.

   b. on a regular basis.

   c. in addition.

10. It is good for a **community** to have employee-owned businesses. A community is

    a. a way to spend money carefully.

    b. a political party that wants strong government.

    c. a group of people living in the same area.

B Read each definition and look at the paragraph number. Look back at the reading on pages 37–38 to find the **boldfaced** word for each definition. Write it in the chart.

Definition	Paragraph	Target Word
1. how good something is	1	
2. cook food inside an oven	1	
3. all the things that affect the place where someone lives or works	7	
4. safety from unwanted change, risk, or loss	7	
5. a group of people chosen to do a particular job or make decisions	8	

DEVELOPING READING SKILLS

Reading for Details

Read these sentences. Then reread "When the Employees Own the Company" for the answers. If the reading doesn't give the information, check (✔) *It doesn't say*.

	True	False	It doesn't say
1. King Arthur has an international market for its flour.	☐	☐	☐
2. Frank and Brinna Sands's children did not want to take charge of King Arthur Flour.	☐	☐	☐
3. King Arthur Flour now has sixteen worker-owners.	☐	☐	☐

	True	False	It doesn't say
4. Some employee-owned businesses produce goods, and others provide services.	☐	☐	☐
5. Worker-owned businesses do not make as much money as traditional businesses.	☐	☐	☐
6. Collective Copies was set up by eight workers who wanted better working conditions.	☐	☐	☐
7. Coamo, Puerto Rico, now has several businesses that are employee-owned.	☐	☐	☐
8. Researchers have studied Italian towns that have worker-owned businesses.	☐	☐	☐

Understanding Topics and Main Ideas

Answer the questions about paragraph topics and main ideas in "When the Employees Own the Company."

A **Write short answers to the questions.**

1. What is the topic of paragraphs 1–3? _____

2. What is the topic of paragraph 4? _____

3. What is the topic of paragraph 5? _____

4. What is the topic of paragraph 7? _____

5. What is the topic of paragraph 8? _____

B **What is the main idea of paragraph 9? Write a complete sentence. Do not copy a sentence from the paragraph. Use your own words.**

_____

_____

EXPANDING VOCABULARY

New Contexts

A Complete the sentences with the target words and phrases in the box. There are two extra words.

baking	besides	profits	quality	security
believing in	organizing	provides	rights	such

1. It is a new business and not yet making any _____.
2. _____ taking four courses, Greta is working fifteen hours a week.
3. A good boss _____ an explanation when making a change.
4. Luis is good at _____ bread.
5. *Cheap* can mean either "not expensive" or "of low _____."
6. A regular schedule can give a child a sense of _____.
7. Alan has to write a twenty-page paper. He has never written _____ a long paper before.
8. Beatriz is _____ the class party. She knows who is bringing what food, who is taking care of the music, and all the other details.

B These sentences also use the target words and phrases **in new contexts.** Complete them with the words and phrases in the box. There are three extra words.

believe in	community	in charge	quality	security
committees	conditions	profits	rights	uncertain

1. Ben volunteered to serve on two _____.
2. Weather _____ were so bad that planes could not land.

3. I _____ giving everyone a chance to give his or her opinion.

4. The fight for women's _____ resulted in women getting the vote.

5. The parents went out and left a babysitter _____.

6. After Ted and Sue had children, they moved to a _____ with good schools.

7. With such _____ economic conditions, it's hard to make business decisions.

Building on the Vocabulary: Word Grammar

A **suffix** is a letter or letters added to the end of a word to make a new word. Look at the words and suffixes in the word family for *employ* ("give a job to"):

employer = a person who gives a job to someone

employee = a person who works for another person, for a company, etc.

employment = work; the fact or condition of having a job

unemployment = the opposite of *employment* (The prefix *un-* means "not" or "the opposite of.")

A Complete the paragraph with the five words from the word family for *employ*. Add *-s* as needed.

The hospital is the biggest _____ in the community. It has
(1)

over 800 _____. It _____ not only doctors and
(2)   (3)

nurses but also managers, office workers, cooks, and so on. Of course, the

hospital is not the only place to find _____ in town. There are
(4)

many jobs available in the area right now, so the _____ rate
(5)

is low.

B **The boldfaced words have the suffixes *-er* and *-ee*. Can you guess their meanings? Write the words next to their definitions.**

a. On the first day at my new job, I met the other **trainees**.

b. Martin is a racehorse **trainer**.

1. _____ = a person who teaches skills, especially for a job or sport

2. _____ = people who are receiving training

Using New Words

Work with a partner. Choose five target words or phrases from the chart on pages 39–40. On a piece of paper, use each word or phrase in a sentence.

Examples:

The future is always <u>uncertain</u>.

A man in my town won the lottery, but most people do not have

<u>such</u> luck.

PUTTING IT ALL TOGETHER

Discussion

Talk about these questions in a small group.

1. What does it mean to say that King Arthur Flour is "an employee-owned, open-book, team-managed company"?

2. What three important ideas do most employee-owned businesses share?

3. The employees at a worker-owned business own a share of their company. How do you think it affects the way they do their jobs?

4. The reading says, "According to a study in Italy, worker-owned businesses are good for their communities." How do you think such businesses help their communities?

Writing

Choose a topic. Write a paragraph.

1. The phrase *working conditions* refers to all the things about your job that affect how you feel about it. They can include everything from the air quality in your workplace to your sense of job security. What working conditions do you think are most important? What does "great working conditions" mean to you? If you wish, you can begin:

   The most important working conditions at a job are . . .

2. Are you good or bad at organizing things? Write about organizing something in your life—for example, your closet, your time on weekends, a party, or a trip.

UNIT 1 Wrap-up

REVIEWING VOCABULARY

 A **Circle the correct words in each group.**

1. Circle the nouns: client customer employee invest political volunteer
2. Circle the verbs: appear bake earn fair hire nature
3. Circle the adjectives: economic huge particular quite uncertain while

 B **Complete the sentences with words and phrases from the box. There are two extra words or phrases.**

believe in	come up with	mean	qualities	set up	take over
besides	deal with	provide	right	sign up	turn into

1. My friends are bringing the food, and I'll _____ the drinks.
2. They don't _____ hitting their children for any reason.
3. At what age do people get the _____ to vote in your country?
4. Clara works fifteen hours a week _____ going to school full-time.
5. Greg hopes his sons will _____ the family business some day.
6. My grandmother has many _____ that I respect.
7. They have to _____ a plan to save the company.
8. I'm sorry, I didn't _____ to step on your foot.
9. How did their discussion _____ a fight?
10. The president _____ a committee to deal with the problem.

EXPANDING VOCABULARY

Word Families

Each form of a word belongs to the same **word family**. For example, the nouns *service* and *server*, the verb *serve*, and the adjective *serviceable* all belong to the same word family.

Two members of a word family may look the same. The words *design*, *drive*, *gain*, *risk*, *screen*, *spread*, and *trade* can be nouns or verbs.

A What part of speech is the **boldfaced** word? Circle *noun* or *verb*.

1. They'll try to keep the new **designs** secret.   *noun*   *verb*

2. Someone so successful must have a lot of **drive**.   *noun*   *verb*

3. They were pleased with the baby's weight **gain**.   *noun*   *verb*

4. The UN peacekeepers **risk** their lives every day.   *noun*   *verb*

5. Do you **screen** your calls or always answer them?   *noun*   *verb*

6. They are working to stop the **spread** of AIDS.   *noun*   *verb*

7. Which countries do they **trade** with most?   *noun*   *verb*

B The **boldfaced** words in these sentences belong to two word families. Write the words in the correct columns in the chart.

	Nouns	Verbs	Adjectives

1. a. Stan works in **advertising**.
   b. The magazine is full of **ads**.
   c. Does every business need to **advertise**?			

2. a. It's a very **profitable** business.
   b. He collects comic books for fun, not **profit**.
   c. Will they **profit** much from the sale?			

A PUZZLE

Complete the sentences with words you studied in Chapters 1–4. Write the words in the puzzle.

Across

3. The cost of health care is a
   m_____ problem.

4. The teacher a_____
   that there would be a test on
   Friday.

6. There are five people on the hiring
   c_____.

9. Is he w_____ to help?

10. He has lived in the same
    c_____ all his life.

11. You'll get your f_____
    share of the profits.

12. Job s_____ means
    fewer worries about the future.

Down

1. Working c_____ were
   very bad, so many employees quit.

2. The housing m_____ is
   strong, and home prices are going
   up.

5. She buys cheap clothes. She
   can't afford anything of high
   q_____.

7. The teachers o_____ a
   trip with the students.

8. W_____ Jack enjoys
   dealing with customers, his
   brother hates it.

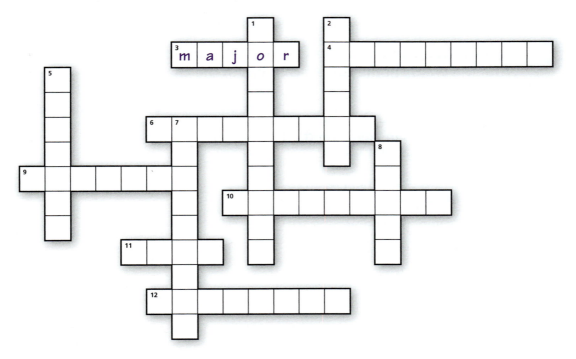

BUILDING DICTIONARY SKILLS

Finding Words in the Dictionary

 Look at these dictionary entries.

> **prof•it¹** /ˈprɑfɪt/ *n* **1** [C,U] Money that you can gain by selling things or doing business: *NovaCorp **made a** pretax **profit** of $39 million. | They sold the company **at a** huge **profit**.* **2** [U] an advantage that you gain from doing something: *reading for profit and pleasure*
> **prof•it²** *v* **1** [I,T] to get something useful or helpful: *Everyone **profits from** an education.* **2** [I] to get money from doing something: *The states have **profited from** cigarette taxes.*

Do you see **profit¹** and **profit²**? The small, raised numbers are called **superscripts**. They tell you that there is more than one entry for *profit*. There are separate entries for the noun and the verb.

Notice superscripts when you look up a word in the dictionary. When there is more than one entry for a word, scan all its meanings and uses.

 A word or phrase often has its own entry in the dictionary. Look at the entry for the adjective *developing*.

> **de•vel•op•ing** /dɪˈvɛləpɪŋ/ *adj* **1** growing or changing: *a developing child* **2 developing countries/nations** poor countries that are trying to increase their industry and trade and improve life for their people

Sometimes words and phrases do not have their own entries. They may appear as part of or following the entry for another word in the same family.

1. Here is the first part of the entry for the noun *charge*. Find and circle the phrase *in charge of*.

> **charge¹** /tʃɑrdʒ/ *n* **1 MONEY** [C,U] the amount of money you have to pay for something: *an admission **charge** of $5 | There's a $70 **charge for** every extra piece of luggage. | We deliver **free of charge** (=at no cost)* **2 CONTROL** [U] the position of having control over or responsibility for something or someone: *Who is **in charge of** the department? | Diane took **charge of** the business when her father died.* **3 CRIME** [C] a statement that says that someone has done something . . .

2. Where in your dictionary would you look for each **boldfaced** phrase? Circle the word you would look up. Then find the phrase in your dictionary.

    a. If you help him out, I'm sure he'll do something for you **in return**.

    b. I cleaned out my closet and **got rid of** clothes I no longer wore.

    c. Yes, you can take the DVDs—**as long as** you promise to return them tomorrow!

    d. Can she really **make a living** as an artist?

3. Find and circle the adjective form of the verb *avoid*.

---

a•void /əˈvɔɪd/ *v* [T] **1** to prevent something bad from happening: *Exercise will help you avoid heart disease.* | *He had to swerve to avoid being hit by the other car.* ⊔Don't say "avoid to do something" t **2** to deliberately stay away from someone or something: *Paul's been avoiding me all day.* **3** to deliberately not do something: *To avoid paying tax, he moved to Canada.* —**avoidable** *adj* —**avoidance** *n* [U]

UNIT
2

HEALTH MATTERS

CHAPTER 5

Living to 100 and Beyond

People today are living longer than ever.

Life expectancy means the number of years a person will probably live. The average life expectancy for a country is how long people in that country usually live. For example, for people in the United States, the average life expectancy is about 78 years. For Canadians, it is about 81.

Talk with a partner or with your class.

1. What do you think the average life expectancy is for people in your country?

2. In what countries do you think people have the longest life expectancy? And the shortest? Why?

3. Do you think life expectancy is the same for both men and women? Tell why or why not.

READING

Look at the words and definitions next to the reading. Then read without stopping. Don't worry about new words. Don't stop to use a dictionary. Just keep reading!

Living to 100 and Beyond

1   Would you like to live to 100? Many people would. Some have dreamed of living even longer—perhaps **forever**. We know this has long been a popular idea because many cultures have legends[1] about ways to avoid growing old.

2   In Europe in the 1400s, people heard stories about a wonderful spring[2] somewhere in eastern Asia. Drinking the water from this spring was supposed to make a person young again. It is **likely** that these stories reached the Spanish explorer[3] Juan Ponce de Léon. Maybe they were on his mind when he traveled to the Americas with Columbus. After arriving in Puerto Rico, Ponce de Léon heard about an island with a **similar** spring, and he decided to go look for it. He invested in three ships, and in 1513, he went searching for the island. However, he ended up in Florida, never finding the island or the spring, which people now call the "Fountain[4] of Youth." When Ponce de Léon died eight years later, he was 61 years old. That may seem young, but it was **actually** a very long life for a man of his times and his way of life.

3   Not long ago, scientists **generally** agreed that the human body could not **possibly** last more than 120 years. Nobody believes 120 to be the **limit** anymore. People have already lived **beyond** that age. A woman in France, Jeanne Louise Calment, **made it** to 122 years and 164 days. People in many parts of the world are living longer lives now than people did in the past, partly because of better public health and safer water supplies. Greater understanding of how to **treat** heart problems has **made a big difference** in life expectancy[5] **as well**. Scientists are learning more all the time about how we can live longer, healthier lives. Maybe someday they will even learn how to stop the aging **process** completely.

(continued)

[1] a *legend* = a well-known story from an earlier time in history

[2] a *spring* = a place where water comes up naturally from the ground

[3] an *explorer* = someone who travels to learn about unknown places

[4] a *fountain*

[5] *life expectancy* = how many years people can expect to live

4   While you are waiting for that day to come, there are things
you can do to increase your life expectancy. You just have to follow
these three simple rules:

5   *Rule #1: Treat your body well.*

Your everyday **lifestyle** influences how long you will live. For
example, smoking can take years off your life. (Even if it does not
make you sick, smoking will affect your skin and make you look
older.) So, do not smoke, get enough sleep, and lead an active life.
Be sure to eat right, too. In other words, eat foods that are good for
you, and do not eat too much.

6   *Rule #2: Do not take risks.*

Forget about motorcycles[6] and take the bus. Wear your seat belt
when you travel by car. Also, choose a nice, safe job. Do not go to
sea and work on a fishing boat—that is a dangerous way to make a
living. If Ponce de Léon had followed Rule #2, he might have lived
many more years. Instead, he ended up fighting Native Americans
in Florida and dying of his **injuries**.

[6] a *motorcycle*

7   *Rule #3: Choose your parents carefully.*

You say this one is not so simple? Well, that is true. However, about
70 percent of your life expectancy depends on your genes,[7] and you
get your genes from your parents. Genes control your hair and eye
color and much, much more. If people in your family usually live
long lives, then chances are good that you will, too.

[7] *your genes* = the
parts of cells in
your body that
control qualities
you get from
your parents

8   It also helps to be born in Australia or Japan, and it helps to be
born female. The average Australian or Japanese man can expect
to see age 79, while his sister can expect to reach 85 or more. Japan
is home to more than 36,000 people who have made it to 100, and
more than 80 percent of them are women.

Quick Comprehension Check

Read these sentences. Circle T (true) or F (false).

1. Many cultures have stories from the past about ways
   to stay young.   T   F

2. Scientists all agree: Nobody can live past 120.   T   F

3. The reading gives "three simple rules" for living longer.   T   F

4. The way you live can add years to your life.   T   F

5. People in certain countries often live longer than
   the average.   T   F

6. How long your family members live has no
   relationship to how long you will.   T   F

EXPLORING VOCABULARY

Thinking about the Target Vocabulary

A Find the four nouns, three verbs, and two adjectives in **bold** in "Living
to 100 and Beyond." Add them to the chart. Write them in the order
they appear in the reading. Use the singular form of any plural noun.
Use the base form of each verb.

	Nouns	Verbs	Adjectives	Other
1				forever
2				
				actually
3				generally
				possibly
				beyond
				as well
5				
6				

B Which words and phrases are new to you? Circle them here. Then find
them in the reading. Look at the context. Can you guess the meaning?

Using the Target Vocabulary

 These sentences are **about the reading**. Complete them with the words and phrases in the box.

forever	likely	made a difference	possibly	similar
lifestyle	limit	made it	process	treat

1. Some people dream of a life without end. They want to live
   _____.

2. Juan Ponce de Léon probably heard the stories from Asia about a spring with special powers. It is _____ that he heard them.

3. He also learned about an island with a _____ spring. The two springs were very much alike.

4. Scientists used to think no one could _____ live more than 120 years. They thought it could not happen in any way.

5. Now, no one thinks of 120 years as the longest anyone can live. No one sees 120 as the _____ anymore.

6. A French woman managed to reach the age of 122. She _____ to 122.

7. Today, doctors know more about heart problems. They can give heart patients new kinds of medical help. They can _____ heart problems better now.

8. Better understanding of heart problems has _____ in many people's life expectancy. It has caused a change for the better.

9. We change as we grow older. We go through the aging _____—that is, we experience a series of changes, actions, or events relating to our minds and bodies.

10. Your _____, or the way you live every day, affects how long you will live.

B Read each definition and look at the paragraph number. Look back at the reading on pages 55–56 to find the **boldfaced** word or phrase to match the definition. Write it in the chart.

Definition	Paragraph	Target Word or Phrase
1. really, truly (but perhaps surprisingly)	2	
2. usually, in most cases	3	
3. past or later than (a certain time or date)	3	
4. too, also	3	
5. hurt done to parts of the body, as in an accident or attack	6	

DEVELOPING READING SKILLS

Understanding and Using Supporting Details

 A Supply a detail from the reading to support each of the general statements below. Use your own words and write complete sentences.

1. People have told many stories about ways to avoid growing old.
   For example, people used to talk about drinking from a "Fountain of Youth."

2. Some people have already lived to be more than 120 years old.
   _____
   _____

3. There are several reasons why people in many countries live longer lives now. _____
   _____
   _____

4. Some things beyond our control affect our life expectancy. _____
   _____
   _____

Write a general statement that relates to each supporting example.

1. <u>Take care of yourself. / Live a healthy lifestyle.</u>

   For example, eat well, exercise, and don't smoke.

2. _____

   For example, take the bus instead of riding a motorcycle.

3. _____

   Don't choose a dangerous career, like working on a fishing boat.

4. _____

   For example, your hair and eye color depend on them, as well as
   about 70 percent of your life expectancy.

5. _____

   For example, people in Japan are more likely to make it to 100.

The Main Idea

**Complete this sentence to give the main idea of "Living to 100 and
Beyond." Write one or more words on each line.**

If you want to _____, then you should
              (1)

_____ and _____, but a lot depends
        (2)   (3)

on your _____, and these you cannot control.
              (4)

EXPANDING VOCABULARY

New Contexts

A **Complete the sentences with the target words and phrases in the box.
There are two extra words.**

actually	lifestyle	limit	possibly	similar
forever	likely	make it	process	treat

1. The speed _____ on this street is 35 miles per hour.

2. The train won't leave for an hour. Don't worry, we'll

   _____ in time.

3. The two companies offer _____ services, so it's hard to choose.

4. I didn't need a doctor. I was able to _____ the cut myself.

5. Getting a college education is a long _____.

6. It's _____ to rain later, so take an umbrella.

7. Everyone calls her Lisa but her name is _____ Elisabeth.

8. The movie had a happy ending. The two main characters promised to love each other _____.

B These sentences also use the target words and phrases **in new contexts. Complete them with the words and phrases in the box. There are three extra words.**

as well	**forever**	**injuries**	**limits**	**possibly**
beyond	**generally**	**lifestyle**	**makes a difference**	**process**

1. Having a baby usually causes changes in a couple's _____.

2. It is _____ believed that money can't buy happiness.

3. With so much about the future uncertain, I can't make plans _____ next week.

4. The job offers good pay and good working conditions _____.

5. People who play sports often have to deal with _____.

6. The fresh paint really _____ in the look of the room.

7. If the rent doubles, then I can't _____ afford it!

Building on the Vocabulary: Word Grammar

> **Adverbs** have many uses. An adverb can modify (or describe):
>
> | | |
> |---|---|
> | a verb | They **worked** quickly. |
> | an adjective | The two plans are quite **similar**. |
> | another adverb | She sings very **well**. |
> | an entire sentence | **Luckily, we made it there on time.** |
>
> The adverb *possibly* usually means "perhaps, maybe": *He's going to buy a car soon, possibly this week.*
>
> When *possibly* follows *can't* or *couldn't*, it means "in any way": *I can't possibly get there today.*

What is the meaning of *possibly* in these sentences? Check (✔) your answers in the chart.

	In any way	Perhaps
1. I'm sorry, but I couldn't possibly go out tonight.		
2. This is possibly your best work ever.		
3. You can't possibly mean what you're saying!		
4. Is it going to rain? Possibly.		

Using New Words

Work with a partner. Choose five target words or phrases from the chart on page 57. On a piece of paper, use each word or phrase in a sentence.

PUTTING IT ALL TOGETHER

Sharing Opinions

Talk about these questions in a small group.

1. Look again at Rules 1, 2, and 3 in the reading. Think about the things these rules say to do. What do you think is simple to do? What is hard?

2. The three rules in the reading say nothing about a person's relationships. Are relationships important in living a long life? Explain your opinion.

3. The three rules say nothing about a person's state of mind—how he or she thinks and feels. Does this have an effect on whether someone lives a long life? Explain your opinion.

4. What do you think the secret is to living a long life?

Writing

Choose a topic. Write a paragraph.

1. Would you like to make it to 100 or beyond? Explain why or why not. If you like, you can begin:

   There are several reasons why I would (not) like to live to be 100.

2. Imagine that today you celebrated your 100th birthday. Now you are writing in your journal about how you spent your day.

The Placebo Effect

CHAPTER 6

Volunteering for a study

GETTING READY TO READ

Talk with a partner or in a small group.

1. When you are sick, what do you usually do? Do you take medicine? Do you see a doctor?

2. When you go to the doctor because you feel sick, do you expect to get a prescription?[1] Explain why or why not.

3. Does a sick person's state of mind (how he or she thinks and feels) affect how quickly the person gets well? Explain your answer.

[1] a *prescription* = a doctor's written order for a specific medicine for a sick person

Look at the picture, words, and definitions next to the reading. Then read without stopping.

The Placebo Effect

1   Harry S. wanted to quit smoking. So, when he saw an ad for a study on ways to **break the habit**, he called and offered to be part of it. The study was at a local university, where Harry and the other volunteers—all of them people who wanted to stop smoking—were divided into three groups. The volunteers in Group A received nicotine gum.[1] (Nicotine is in tobacco.[2] It is what gives smokers the good feeling they get from smoking.) When these smokers felt the need for a cigarette, they could **chew** a piece of this gum instead. It would give them the nicotine they were used to. The volunteers in Group B, including Harry, got some gum, too. It was just **plain** chewing gum, but the volunteers did not know that. The people in Group C got nothing. (A group like this in a study is called *the control group*.)

2   After a four-hour period with no cigarettes, Harry and the other volunteers had to write answers to a set of questions. Their answers showed how badly they wanted a cigarette. Not surprisingly, the smokers in Group C—the control group, which got no gum—showed the strongest cravings.[3] The smokers in the other two groups did not feel such a strong need to smoke.

3   What surprised the researchers was that the results for Groups A and B were exactly the same. That meant that the plain chewing gum worked as well as the gum with nicotine. Why? The researchers say, "Maybe it was the placebo effect." In other words, the smokers in Group B believed the gum would help them feel better, so they did feel better.

4   A placebo is something that seems like a medical **treatment** but provides no real medicine. The word *placebo* means "I will please" in Latin. Doctors sometimes give a placebo to please a patient who does not really need medicine but wants some.

5   Not everyone believes that the placebo effect **exists**, but researchers in Houston, Texas, found some interesting evidence[4] for it. They did a study on a common—and expensive—type of knee **operation**. About 350,000 people a year have this surgery.[5] The 180 volunteers in the study all understood that they might get a real

(continued)

[1] a pack of *gum*

[2] *tobacco* = the plant whose leaves are used to make cigarettes and cigars

[3] a *craving* = a very strong wish for something (such as a certain food)

[4] *evidence* = facts that show something is true

[5] *surgery* = when a doctor cuts open the body to fix or take out something; an operation

knee operation or they might not. The ones who had **fake** surgery got only three small cuts around their knee (to make it look real). After two weeks, most patients believed that their surgery had been real. Later, 35–40 percent of the patients who actually had surgery reported that their knees felt better. Among those who had the "placebo surgery," the **percentage** who felt better was the same. In other words, the fake (and cheaper) operation had helped people just as much as the real one.

6   Some researchers think that the placebo effect works only in a very few **situations**, possibly only in the case of pain. They have an idea how it works in such cases. **Recent** studies show that when patients believe that they are getting treatment and that their pain will go away, their brains produce natural painkillers. The brain's own painkillers then help **block** the pain.

7   The smokers in Harry's group felt fewer cravings than expected, and the fake surgery patients felt less knee pain than expected. In both cases, maybe just the idea of getting treatment (a supply of nicotine or an operation) **had something to do with** the results. Or perhaps something else was happening. For example, maybe the sugar in the chewing gum helped Harry and the others in his group feel better. Scientists agree that **further** research is needed. **So far**, no one has really **proven** that the placebo effect exists.

Quick Comprehension Check

Read these sentences. Circle T (true) or F (false).

1. Harry's doctor made him be part of a study on quitting smoking.   T   F

2. Chewing gum helped the smokers go without smoking.   T   F

3. A placebo has strong drugs in it.   T   F

4. The placebo effect depends on what a person believes.   T   F

5. Doctors have done only one study on the placebo effect.   T   F

6. The brain can produce its own painkillers.   T   F

EXPLORING VOCABULARY

Thinking about the Target Vocabulary

 Find the four nouns, six verbs, and four adjectives in **bold** in "The Placebo Effect." Add them to the chart. Use the singular form of any plural noun. Use the base form of each verb.

	Nouns	Verbs	Adjectives	Other
1				
4				
5				
6				
7				
			so far	

 Which words and phrases are new to you? Circle them here. Then find them in the reading. Look at the context. Can you guess the meaning?

Using the Target Vocabulary

 These sentences are about the reading. Complete them with the words and phrases in the box.

blocks	exist	situations
break the habit	had something to do with	treatment
chew	operation	

1. For Harry, smoking was a thing he did repeatedly. He wanted to stop doing it. He wanted to _____ of smoking.

2. Some of the volunteers in the smoking study got gum to _____. This word means "bite food (or gum) in your mouth again and again."

3. When doctors take action to help a patient with a sickness or injury, they are giving the patient medical _____.

4. Some people believe there is no such thing as the placebo effect. They say that the placebo effect doesn't really _____.

5. Researchers in Texas did a study on a common knee _____. This word refers to the process of cutting into someone's body to repair or remove something.

6. Doctors give placebos to patients in certain _____, meaning when certain conditions are present or when certain things are happening.

7. When a painkiller stops pain from traveling through the body to the brain, you can say it _____ the pain.

8. The volunteers who got chewing gum thought they would feel less of a need for a cigarette. Maybe that idea had a role in, or was related to, their experience. Maybe that idea _____ their results.

B   These sentences are also **about the reading**. What is the meaning of each **boldfaced** word or phrase? Circle a, b, or c.

1. Some of the volunteers in the smoking study got just **plain** chewing gum. In this sentence, *plain* means
   a. special.
   b. with nothing added.
   c. high-quality.

2. Some patients had **fake** surgery—only three small cuts around their knee. *Fake* tells us that their operations were
   a. not painful.
   b. not expensive.
   c. not real.

3. What **percentage** of the patients said they felt better? A *percentage* is
   a. a particular amount out of every 100.
   b. a group of similar people.
   c. a medical researcher.

4. There have been **recent** studies showing that what a patient believes affects his or her pain. *Recent* means happening
   a. a little while ago.
   b. without pay.
   c. accidentally.

5. Scientists say that **further** research is needed. *Further* means
   a. international.
   b. more, additional.
   c. uncertain.

6. **So far**, there has been no general agreement about the placebo effect. *So far* means
   a. possibly.
   b. happily.
   c. until now.

7. No one has **proven** that the placebo effect exists. *Prove something* means to
   a. doubt that it is real.
   b. show it clearly.
   c. sign up for it.

DEVELOPING READING SKILLS

Quoting and Paraphrasing

When you **quote** someone, you repeat the person's exact words. Use quotation marks (" ") to mark the beginning and the end of the quotation.

A placebo "seems like a medical treatment but provides no real medicine."

When you **paraphrase**, you say the same thing as someone else but in a different way.

If someone is getting a placebo, that means he thinks he is getting medical treatment but he isn't actually getting any medicine.

 A The following sentences paraphrase sentences in the reading. Find the sentence in the reading with the same meaning and copy it here. Use quotation marks (" ") because you are quoting someone else's exact words.

1. The researchers were surprised to see Groups A and B show the same results. "What surprised the researchers was that the results for Groups A and B were exactly the same."

2. Harry S. was a smoker who wanted to break the habit. _____
   _____

3. The volunteers in all three groups spent four hours without smoking and then had to answer some questions. _____
   _____

4. Scientists think that they need to study the placebo effect some more. _____
   _____

5. Up to now, no one has shown that there really is such a thing as the placebo effect. _____
   _____

There are two main ways to **paraphrase**:

- Change words and phrases to other words and phrases with similar meanings.
- Change the order of the parts of a sentence or the way the information is organized in a sentence.

B **Complete the chart with examples of ways to paraphrase from Part A.**

Two Main Ways to Paraphrase	Examples of Paraphrasing from Part A	
	Change From	**To**
• Change words and phrases. Use synonyms.	2. "quit smoking"	a smoker/break the habit
	4. "further research is needed"	
	5. "proven"	
• Change the way sentences are organized.	1. "What surprised the researchers was that the results for . . ."	The researchers were surprised to see Groups A and B show . . .
	3. "After a four-hour period with no cigarettes, Harry and the other volunteers . . ."	

Understanding Reference Words

> A **reference word** takes the place of a noun or a noun phrase. Pronouns, such as *he*, *she*, *it*, and *them*, are reference words. The words *one*, *ones*, *this*, *that*, *these*, and *those* can also be reference words. Reference words refer back to someone or something already named.

What do the boldfaced pronouns mean in these sentences? Look back at the reading.

1. Paragraph 1: . . . he called and offered to be part of **it**. _____

2. Paragraph 1: **It** is what gives smokers the good feeling they get . . .
   _____

3. Paragraph 3: **That** meant that the plain chewing gum worked . . .
   _____

4. Paragraph 5: . . . researchers in Houston, Texas, have found some interesting evidence for **it**. _____

5. Paragraph 5: The **ones** who had fake surgery . . . _____

6. Paragraph 5: . . . just as much as the real **one**. _____

Summarizing

Complete this summary paragraph to give the main ideas of "The Placebo Effect." If you copy from the reading (groups of more than a few words), then use quotation marks.

According to "The Placebo Effect," a placebo is _____
                                                              (1)
_____. The term *the placebo effect* refers

to someone feeling better when he or she believes _____
                                                                     (2)

_____ but _____
                                                              (3)

_____. Researchers who have studied the

placebo effect agree that _____
                                                         (4)

_____.

EXPANDING VOCABULARY

New Contexts

A   **Complete the sentences with the target words and phrases in the box. There are two extra words.**

block	further	plain	recent	so far
break the habit	percentage	prove	situation	treatment

1. She is still in pain from a _____ operation.

2. I wish he would _____ of calling me every time he has a problem.

3. We haven't had any trouble yet. Everything has gone smoothly _____.

4. He prefers _____ pizza: just cheese and tomato sauce, nothing else.

5. The new manager still has to _____ that he can do the job.

6. We had a good meeting. We'll make a decision after _____ discussion tomorrow.

7. Doctors are working on a new _____ for patients with burns.

8. What is the political _____ in the country at the moment?

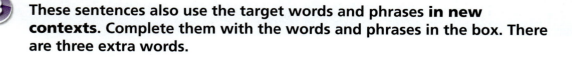

B These sentences also use the target words and phrases **in new contexts**. Complete them with the words and phrases in the box. There are three extra words.

block	exist	has something to do with	percentage	recent
chew	fake	operation	plain	situation

1. The _____ took hours, but the patient is doing well.
2. One of my teeth hurts, so I can't _____ on that one side of my mouth.
3. His most recent book _____ Mexican history, I think.
4. When trees come down during a storm, they sometimes _____ roads.
5. A large _____ of U.S. high school students have jobs.
6. Dinosaurs[1] no longer _____.
7. When the police caught him, he had several _____ IDs.[2]

[1] *Dinosaurs* lived millions of years ago.   [2] An *ID* is an identification card.

Building on the Vocabulary: Word Grammar

> *Farther* and *further* are both comparative forms of *far*. In conversation, many people use either one; in writing, follow these rules.
>
> - Use *farther* when you mean a longer distance: *They ran farther than we did.*
> - Use *further* when you refer to time, amounts, or processes: *We need to study the problem further.*
>
> These words can be adjectives (*the farther star, further research*) or adverbs (*it spread farther, we didn't discuss it any further*).

 A **Complete the sentences with *farther* or *further*.**

1. My classroom is _____ down the hall.
2. I need _____ practice.
3. They never developed the plan any _____.
4. Clear Lake is nicer than Heart Lake, but it's _____ away.
5. You can swim _____ than I can.
6. He will study math _____ when he goes to college.

 B **Write your own sentences using *farther* and *further*.**

1. _____
2. _____

Using New Words

Work with a partner. Choose five target words or phrases from the chart on page 67. On a piece of paper, use each word or phrase in a sentence.

PUTTING IT ALL TOGETHER

Discussion

Talk about these questions in a small group.

1. What was the purpose of the first study described in the reading? How were the three groups different? What surprised the researchers and why?

2. What was the purpose of the second study? How were the two groups of patients different? What were the results?

3. Imagine that you are invited to be part of a study on a new drug. The drug is supposed to strengthen a person's memory and make him or her smarter. Some of the volunteers will get the drug, and some will get a placebo. Would you volunteer to be part of the study? Explain your answer.

Writing

Choose a topic. Write a paragraph.

1. Answer question 3 from **Discussion** above. If you wish, you can begin:

   Researchers working on a new drug have invited me to be part of a study. The drug is designed to make people smarter and give them stronger memories. As a volunteer, I might get the drug, or I might get a placebo. I have decided . . .

2. When do you go to see a doctor? How do you feel about going to doctors?

CHAPTER 7

Tears

Chopping onions may make you cry.

GETTING READY TO READ

Talk with a partner or in a small group.

1. When was the last time you cried? Why did you cry?

2. When is it OK to cry? Are there times when a person *should* cry?

3. Do you agree with a, b, or c? Choose one and explain your choice.

   a. Crying is a healthy thing to do.

   b. Crying is bad for you.

   c. Crying is neither good for you nor bad for you.

READING

Look at the words and definitions next to the reading. Then read without stopping.

Tears

1   Tears are good for your eyes. In fact, without them, your eyes would not even be able to move. Some people say tears help us in other ways, too. Maybe you know someone who likes to watch sad movies in order to "have a good cry." It has not been proven, but tears may be good not only for your eyes but for your **emotional** health as well.

2   We generally notice tears only when we cry, but we have them in our eyes all the time. Tears affect how we see the world while at the same time protecting our eyes from it. Without this **liquid** covering them, our eyes would be at risk of infection.[1] We also need tears in order to see. The cornea[2] of the eye does not have a perfectly smooth **surface**. Tears **fill in** the holes in the cornea and make it smooth so that we can see clearly. Without tears, the world would look very strange to us.

3   There are three types of tears, called *basal*, *reflex*, and *emotional* (or *psychic*) tears. These three types **differ** not only in purpose but also in composition.[3]

4   • Basal tears are the ones that we produce all the time. On average, our eyes produce these tears at a rate of five to ten ounces[4] a day. When we **blink**, we spread basal tears across the surface of our eyes. If we do not blink often enough, like some people who spend long hours in front of a computer, then our eyes get dry.

5   • Have you ever cut up an onion and felt tears come to your eyes? Tears of that type are called reflex tears. They are the ones that fill our eyes when a cold wind **blows**. These tears also protect our eyes, washing away dust and other **materials** that get into them.

6   • Emotional, or psychic, tears **flow** when we feel certain emotions. When we cry tears of sadness, disappointment, or happiness, we are crying emotional tears. Emotional tears are the tears we think of when we use the word *cry*.

7   Tom Lutz, the author of *Crying: The Natural and Cultural History of Tears,* writes, "**Throughout** history, and in every culture, . . . everyone, everywhere cries at some time." Even men and women

[1] *infection* = sickness in a part of the body

[2] the *cornea* = a covering for the eye; see the picture on page 79

[3] *composition* = the way something is made up of different things, parts, etc.

[4] an *ounce* = a small amount of liquid (less than 0.03 liters)

who say they never cry can usually remember crying as children. Most of us probably think it is **normal** for men or women to cry at certain times. For example, it is no surprise when someone cries during a sad movie, and we often expect people to cry when a family member dies. At such times, we may even tell them to "**go ahead** and cry." However, we do not always take this **view** of tears. Sometimes adults who cry—or even children who do—lose the respect of others. What would you think, for example, of an adult who cried over losing a card game? Most people are aware of the social rules about when, where, and why it is acceptable[5] to cry. These rules generally differ for children and adults, and often for men and women. They depend on things such as family, culture, and religion, and they change over time.

[5] *acceptable =* generally considered good enough (behavior)

8   Some people think it is not just acceptable to cry but actually healthy to let the tears flow. Doctors in Greece over 2,500 years ago thought that tears came from the brain and that everyone needed to let them out. Today, many people still believe in getting tears out. They say that through crying, we get rid of emotions we have stored up, which is good for our **mental** health. Some people report that they feel better after crying. This could be because of the **chemicals** in emotional tears. One chemical is a type of endorphin, a painkiller that the body naturally produces. Emotional tears increase the amount of endorphin that gets to the brain because tears flow from the eye into the nose and pass to the brain that way. This painkiller may make a person less aware of sad or angry feelings, and that could explain why someone feels better after "a good cry."

Front view of an eye

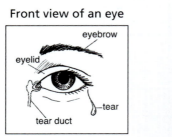

Side view of an eye

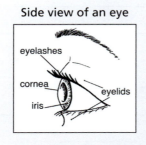

_____

Tom Lutz's words come from *Crying: The Natural and Cultural History of Tears* (New York: W. W. Norton & Company, 1999), 17.

Quick Comprehension Check

Read these sentences. Circle T (true) or F (false).

1. Tears are important for keeping our eyes healthy.　　　　　T　F

2. Tears are important for our ability to see.　　　　　T　F

3. There are two different kinds of tears.　　　　　T　F

4. We have emotional tears in our eyes all the time.　　　　　T　F

5. People generally have the same ideas about when it is OK to cry.　　　　　T　F

6. Some people think it can be good for you to cry.　　　　　T　F

EXPLORING VOCABULARY

Thinking about the Target Vocabulary

(A) **Find the five nouns, six verbs, and three adjectives in bold in "Tears." Add them to the chart. Use the singular form of any plural noun. Use the base form of each verb.**

	Nouns	Verbs	Adjectives	Other
1				
2				
3				
4				
5				

	Nouns	Verbs	Adjectives	Other
6				
7				throughout
8				

B Which words and phrases are new to you? Circle them here. Then find them in the reading. Look at the context. Can you guess the meaning?

Using the Target Vocabulary

A These sentences are **about the reading**. What is the meaning of each **boldfaced** word or phrase? Circle a, b, or c.

1. Tears may be good for your **emotional** health. *Your emotional health* means the condition of your
   a. body.
   b. eyes.
   c. mind and feelings.

2. Your eye does not have a smooth **surface**. Like your skin, your eye has tiny holes and wrinkles. The surface of something is
   a. its top, outer layer.
   b. the inside of it.
   c. the color of it.

3. You spread tears across your eyes when you **blink**. *Blink* means
   a. cry.
   b. take a nap.
   c. open and close your eyes quickly.

4. We may think it is **normal** for people to cry at certain times. *Normal* means
   a. surprising.
   b. usual, expected.
   c. strange and funny.

5. You might tell someone, "**Go ahead** and cry." Saying *go ahead and* (do something) tells the person
   a. that it's OK to do it.
   b. to follow you.
   c. to hurry up.

These sentences are also about the reading. Complete them with the words and phrases in the box.

blows	differ	flow	materials	throughout
chemicals	fill them in	liquid	mental	views

1. Tears are like water. They are a _____ (not a solid or a gas).

2. The surface of your eye has tiny holes. You need tears to _____ and make the cornea smooth so that you can see clearly.

3. The three types of tears are not the same. They _____ in purpose and in composition.

4. When a wind _____ cold air into your eyes, they fill with reflex tears.

5. Tears help wash away dust, dirt, sand, or any other _____ that might get into your eyes.

6. When you feel certain emotions, tears may start to _____, like water moving in a river.

7. According to Tom Lutz, people in every culture, at every point _____ history, have cried.

8. People don't all share the same opinions about tears. People hold different _____ .

9. Tears are good for your eyes and may be good for your _____ health, too, meaning your state of mind and the way you think.

10. There are different substances in the three types of tears. The _____ in emotional tears include a painkiller.

DEVELOPING READING SKILLS

Quoting and Paraphrasing

 A **Answer each question by copying a sentence from "Tears." Use quotation marks (" ") before and after the sentence.**

1. What would happen if we did not have tears in our eyes?
   "Without this liquid covering them, our eyes would be at risk of infection."

2. How do tears help us see clearly?

3. What are the different types of tears?

4. Social rules about crying differ for children versus adults and often for men versus women. What else affects the rules?

5. What is a possible effect of the painkiller endorphin?

B **One sentence in each pair paraphrases the sentence from the reading. Circle the correct answer.**

1. It has not been proven, but tears may be good not only for your eyes but for your emotional health as well.
   a. No one knows if tears are actually good for your eyes or for your emotions.
   b. Tears are good for our eyes and may be good for our emotional health, too.

2. Emotional tears are the tears we think of when we use the word *cry*.
   a. The word *cry* refers to one kind of tears, emotional tears.
   b. We cry emotional tears when we think of the word *cry*.

3. Most people are aware of the social rules about when, where, and why it is acceptable to cry.

  a. Sometimes it is OK to cry, and sometimes it is not, and you have to learn the difference.

  b. Each culture has its rules for when crying is OK, and most members of a culture know its rules.

 C **On a piece of paper, write answers to these questions. Do not copy sentences from the reading—paraphrase them. (Remember: There are examples of ways to paraphrase on page 83.)**

1. How do tears help our eyes?

2. When do our eyes produce basal, reflex, and emotional tears?

3. Why do some people believe it is good to cry?

Summarizing

On a piece of paper, write a one-paragraph summary of "Tears." Include the answers to the questions below. Try to paraphrase. Use quotation marks as needed. If you wish, you can begin:

The reading "Tears" gives several reasons why tears are good for us.

• What are tears good for?

• Which kinds of tears protect our eyes?

• Which kind of tears do we produce when we cry?

• What do social rules about crying tell us?

• What do some people believe about crying?

EXPANDING VOCABULARY

New Contexts

 A **Complete the sentences with the target words and phrases in the box. There are two extra words.**

blew	differs	go ahead	mental
blinked	emotional	liquid	normal
chemicals	flows	materials	surface

1. The river _____ to the sea.

2. Only a few people have walked on the _____ of the moon.

3. A strong wind _____ the man's hat off.

4. My photo didn't turn out well because I _____.

5. Ann says, "I have a _____ block against math. I don't understand it or enjoy it, and I never will."

6. It's _____ to feel nervous during a job interview. Everyone does.

7. To build a good house, you need good-quality building _____.

8. _____ and take the last piece of pizza.

9. You can depend on your friends for _____ support in difficult times.

10. There are strong _____ in some cleaning products.

B Read these sentences. Write the **boldfaced** target words or phrases next to their definitions. There is one extra definition. Put an X next to it.

a. Water can take the form of a **liquid**, a gas, or a solid (ice).

b. I cried **throughout** the movie, from beginning to end.

c. The two companies **differ** in how they treat their employees.

d. Who did he vote for? Do you know his political **views**?

e. There is a bad hole in the street. Somebody should **fill it in**.

Target Words or Phrases   **Definitions**

1. _____ = be different or not alike

2. _____ = opinions or beliefs

3. _____ = during all of a period of time

4. _____ = open or empty spaces in something solid

5. _____ = a substance that can flow and be poured

6. _____ = put something in a hole in order to make a smooth surface

Building on the Vocabulary: Studying Collocations

> The noun *view* has different meanings:
>
> - *View* often means "opinion, belief." Use *take* or *hold* with *view* to mean "have an opinion": *He takes the view that children should be seen and not heard.*
>
> - *View* can also mean "the area someone can see." Use *have* with *view* when it has this meaning: *He has a view of the park from his house.*

 Complete the following sentences. Make true statements.

1. _____ and I hold similar views on _____.
   (name)

2. From my _____ window, I have a view of _____.
   (room)

 On a piece of paper, write two more sentences with *view*.

Using New Words

Work with a partner. Choose five target words or phrases from the chart on pages 80–81. On a piece of paper, use each word or phrase in a sentence.

PUTTING IT ALL TOGETHER

Sharing Opinions

1. Check (✓) your answers to questions a–f on page 87. Add a situation of your own to the list. Then share answers with a partner. Ask your partner about the situation you added.

Is it OK for a person to cry:

	An Adult		A Child	
	Yes	No	Yes	No
a. at the movies?				
b. when his/her team loses a game?				
c. when something bad happens at work/at school?				
d. when saying good-bye at the airport?				
e. at a religious service for someone who has died?				
f. _____?				

2. How does a person learn the social rules about crying?

3. Do you think there are differences between the social rules about crying for men and those for women? Fill in the diagram with situations. Compare charts with your partner.

When is it OK to cry?

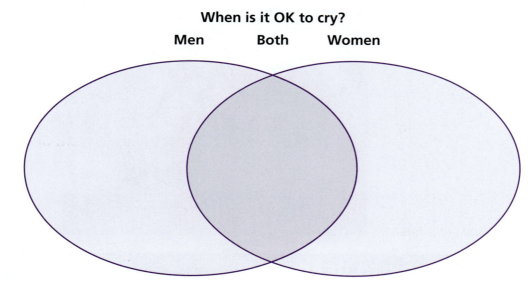

Men   Both   Women

Writing

Choose a topic. Write a paragraph.

1. Do you remember crying as a child, or a recent experience that made you cry? Describe it.

2. Write about one of the opinions you expressed in **Sharing Opinions** above. Give your reasons for what you believe.

Bionic Men and Women

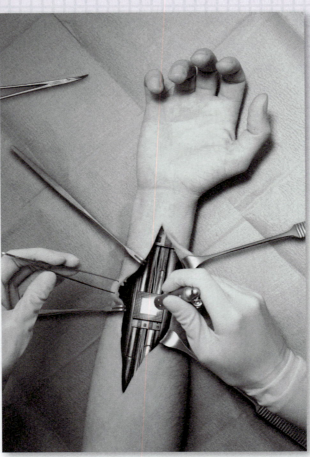

A hand of the future?

GETTING READY TO READ

Talk in a small group or with your class.

1. What movies or TV shows have you seen about a person who was part machine? What was the story about?

2. When a part of someone's body stops working, the person's life may depend on a machine, whether in the hospital or in everyday life. Give an example of a situation like this.

READING

Look at the pictures, words, and definitions next to the reading. Then read without stopping.

Bionic Men and Women

1   In the movie *Star Wars: The Empire Strikes Back*, Luke Skywalker loses a hand but gets a new one, an **artificial** hand that looks and works just like a real one. This is not unusual in sci-fi[1] movies that take place far into the future. It is easy to believe that 100 years from now, doctors will be able to **replace** parts of the body with machines. But you do not have to go to the movies to see this happen.

2   Machines are already doing the jobs of various parts of the human body. There are people who can see, hear, walk, or pick up their children because of artificial eyes, ears, legs, and arms. These are all possible because of **developments** in the field of bionics. *Bionics* means the study of how living things are made and how they work. **Engineers** study bionics to design machines that are similar to living things. For example, in order to design airplanes, engineers have studied birds. The field of bionics also includes building machines to replace parts of the body or to support processes **within** the body.

3   One example of a bionic device[2] is the pacemaker. A pacemaker can help someone whose heart **beats** too slowly or not **regularly** enough. The device goes into the person's **chest** and is **attached** to the heart with wires. The wires carry small amounts of electricity to the heart from a **battery**. That keeps the heart beating as it should.

4   Other bionic devices, like Luke Skywalker's new hand, take the place of a part of the body. A major problem in developing bionic devices has been setting up communication between the body and the machine. Normally, the brain tells parts of the body what to do by sending messages along nerves.[3] For example, your brain might send a message to your hand telling it to pick up a pen and write. But how would it tell an artificial hand to do that? Dr. William Craelius, who has invented an artificial hand, says, "Communication is **key**, and it is getting easier."

5   Machines are not the only things that can replace a part of the body. A transplant is an operation to move a body part, such as a heart or a kidney,[4] from one person to another. One major problem

(continued)

[1] *sci-fi* = (informal) *science fiction*, stories about imaginary worlds or future developments in science

[2] a *device* = a small machine or tool that does a special job

[3] *nerves* = thin parts like lines throughout the body that carry information to/ from the brain

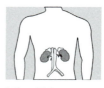

[4] the *kidneys*

with transplants is a lack[5] of available hearts, kidneys, and so on, so hospitals cannot **keep up with** the **demand**. Patients have to wait, and some patients have no time left. **Therefore**, many scientists see bionics as the best hope for the future. Using bionics, a patient could get a new heart or kidney right away instead of waiting for a transplant. Other scientists disagree. They say that bionics is already a thing of the past, and they have a better idea: They are working on using animal parts for transplants.

6   Maybe in the future our choices will not be limited to bionic devices and transplant operations. Maybe science will take us in another direction. Consider the salamader:[6] If it loses a leg, it can grow a new one. What if a person who lost a hand or a kidney could grow a new one? This may sound like something from another sci-fi movie, but it could happen. Researchers are studying the genes[7] that let salamanders grow new legs, and they hope to learn how human beings might do the same thing.

7   Growing a new part of the body could be the best way to go. On the other hand, some people, if they had the choice, might prefer bionic devices. In sci-fi movies, you may have seen people become cyborgs—half human being, half machine—with bionic parts that give them special powers, such as super-human speed or **strength**. Think about it. If bionics could turn you into a superman, what would you do?

———
Dr. Craelius's words come from the article "Inventor of Artificial Hand Sees 'Bionic' Replacement Parts Becoming More Human," *Medical Devices & Surgical Technology Week* (March 10, 2002), 3.

[5] a *lack* = not having something or not having enough of it

[6] a *salamander*

[7] *genes* = the parts of cells in your body that control qualities you get from your parents

Quick Comprehension Check

Read these sentences. Circle T (true) or F (false).

1. People can get new body parts only in the movies.   T   F

2. Bionics means studying living things—how they are made and how they work.   T   F

3. Giving a man a pacemaker for his heart is an example of using bionics.   T   F

4. Machines are our only hope for new body parts in the future.   T   F

5. Some animals can grow new body parts if they need to.   T   F

6. In the movies, bionic body parts sometimes give people special abilities.   T   F

 EXPLORING VOCABULARY

Thinking about the Target Vocabulary

A Find the six nouns, four verbs, and two adjectives in **bold** in "Bionic Men and Women." Add them to the chart. Use the singular form of any plural nouns. Use the base form of each verb.

	Nouns	Verbs	Adjectives	Other
1				
2				
				within
3				
				regularly
4				
5				
				therefore
7				

B   Which words and phrases are new to you? Circle them in the chart on page 91. Then find them in the reading. Look at the context. Can you guess the meaning?

Using the Target Vocabulary

A   Complete these sentences **about the reading**. Use the words and phrases in the box.

beats	developments	keep up with	replace
chest	engineers	regularly	strength

1. In movies, doctors of the future can take a part of the body that is injured or not working and put a machine in its place. The doctors _____ parts of the body.

2. There have been changes in the field of bionics, changes for the better. These _____ in the field have made new devices possible.

3. The people who study bionics so that they can design better machines are _____.

4. A healthy heart makes slow, steady movements when it is at rest. It _____ slowly.

5. A healthy heart beats with the same amount of time between each movement and the next. It beats _____.

6. A pacemaker is a bionic device that goes into a person's _____ (the part of the body where your heart is).

7. Hospitals cannot do as many transplant operations as are needed because of the limited supply of hearts, kidneys, and so on. Hospitals cannot _____ the demand for transplants.

8. In sci-fi movies, sometimes a man becomes very strong after an operation makes him half man and half machine. His bionic devices give him superhuman _____.

B These sentences are also **about the reading.** What is the meaning of each **boldfaced** word or phrase? Circle a, b, or c.

1. Some people have to get **artificial** eyes, ears, hands, and legs. *Artificial* means
   a. not available. b. not natural. c. not connected.

2. A machine may be needed to support a process **within** the body. *Within* means
   a. beyond. b. according to. c. inside.

3. Doctors **attach** a pacemaker to a heart with wires. *Attach* means
   a. block. b. connect. c. avoid.

4. A pacemaker gets its power from a **battery**. A battery provides
   a. software. b. electricity. c. treatment.

5. The body and the bionic device must communicate. Communication is **key**. *Key* means
   a. worth nothing. b. not likely. c. needed for success.

6. There is a great **demand** for transplants. *Demand* means
   a. the lifestyle people want. b. the materials people use. c. the need people have.

7. Transplants aren't always possible when patients need them. **Therefore**, some people think bionics offers more hope for the future. *Therefore* means
   a. right away. b. because. c. for that reason.

DEVELOPING READING SKILLS

Quoting and Paraphrasing

Answer these questions about "Bionic Men and Women" on a piece of paper. Try to paraphrase sentences from the reading. If you quote more than a few words, use quotation marks around the material copied from the reading.

1. What does *bionics* mean?
2. What is a pacemaker? What does it do?

3. Why has it been so hard to develop things like artificial hands?

4. What is a transplant operation?

5. What is one problem with transplants?

6. Why are researchers studying salamanders?

7. Why might some people like the idea of getting bionic body parts?

Text Organization

Complete the diagram. Write notes about the information found in the reading.

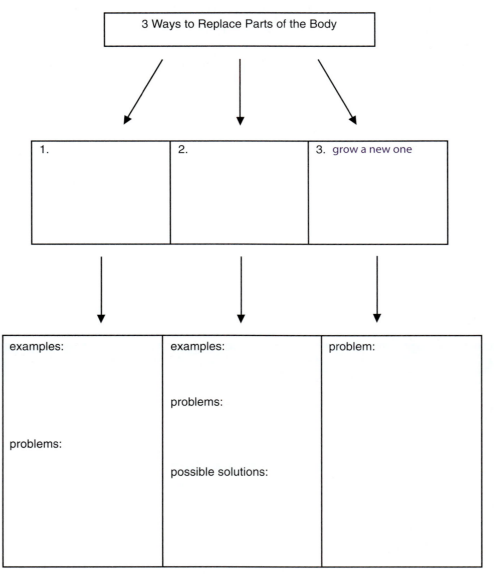

Summarizing

On a piece of paper, write a one-paragraph summary of "Bionic Men and Women." Include the answers to the questions below. Try to paraphrase. Use quotation marks as needed. If you wish, you can begin:

The reading "Bionic Men and Women" describes developments in the field of bionics.

- What does *bionics* mean?
- How do bionic devices help people?
- What is another way to replace a part of the body that isn't working?
- What other way to replace body parts may be possible in the future?

EXPANDING VOCABULARY

New Contexts

A **Complete the sentences with the target words and phrases in the box. There are two extra words or phrases.**

artificial	beat	keep up with	strength
attach	demand	key	therefore
battery	development	regularly	within

1. After being sick, I hardly had the _____ to get out of bed.
2. Please _____ a recent photo to your application.
3. Those _____ flowers look real, don't they?
4. Our hotel was _____ walking distance of the city center.
5. My camera isn't working. It needs a new _____.
6. His heart _____ faster when he saw her.
7. The _____ thing is for the patient to believe in the treatment.
8. Parents, make sure your children brush their teeth _____!
9. The plan presented too many risks. _____, he decided against it.
10. The company went out of business because there wasn't enough _____ for their products.

Read these sentences. Write the boldfaced target words or phrases next to their definitions. There is one extra definition. Put an X next to it.

a. They want to **replace** their old car.

b. Recent **developments** in medical research give us reason to hope.

c. **Engineers** are employed in many different fields.

d. The young father held his baby against his **chest**.

e. We couldn't **keep up with** the other runners, so we gave up.

**Target Words
or Phrases   Definitions**

1. _____ = fix, repair

2. _____ = change (one person or thing for another)

3. _____ = changes that make something more advanced

4. _____ = people who design machines, roads, bridges, etc.

5. _____ = move as fast or do as much (as someone else)

6. _____ = the front part of a person's body between the neck
and the stomach

Building on the Vocabulary: Studying Collocations

Certain prepositions often follow certain nouns, verbs, and adjectives. Use:

n. + prep.	v. + prep.	adj. + prep.
demand **for**	attach something **to**	key **to**
injury **to**	differ **from**	normal **for**
treatment **for**	replace something **with**	similar **to**

 Complete each sentence with a preposition.

1. Certain players have been key _____ the success of the team.

2. There is an increased demand _____ biomedical engineers.

3. The child's eating habits are normal _____ his age.

4. Her situation is similar _____ yours.

5. He wants to replace his desktop computer _____ a laptop.

6. Is he getting treatment _____ his heart problem?

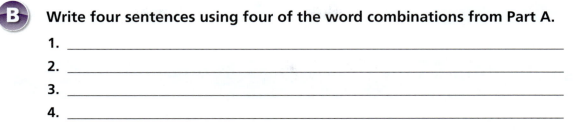 **B** Write four sentences using four of the word combinations from Part A.

1. _____

2. _____

3. _____

4. _____

Using New Words

Work with a partner. Choose five target words or phrases from the chart on page 91. On a piece of paper, use each word or phrase in a sentence.

PUTTING IT ALL TOGETHER

Role-play

Form a small group. Two of you are scientists. You work in the field of bionics. The rest of you are reporters, and you are here to interview the scientists about the most recent developments in their work. The reporters ask questions. The scientists answer the questions and can ask their own questions. If you wish, you can begin:

REPORTER: What are you working on right now?

SCIENTIST: We are developing a new . . .

Writing

Choose a topic. Write a paragraph.

1. Imagine that you could replace some part or parts of your body with artificial part(s) that would give you super powers, special powers that human beings don't normally have. What would you replace and why? If you wish, you can begin:

    If I could, I would replace my . . .

2. Would you like a career as a designer or an engineer? Explain.

REVIEWING VOCABULARY

A **Complete the phrase.**

1. Write the adjective *emotional, likely, plain,* or *similar.*

   a. the _____ result

   b. an _____ good-bye

   c. _____ lifestyles

   d. _____ food

2. Write the noun *chest, engineers, percentage,* or *treatments.*

   a. a high _____

   b. highly trained _____

   c. painful _____

   d. a hairy _____

3. Write the adjective *artificial, further, mental,* or *smooth.*

   a. _____ health

   b. _____ flowers

   c. _____ developments

   d. _____ surfaces

B Complete the sentences with words or phrases in the box. There are two extra words or phrases.

actually	go ahead	make it
as well	has nothing to do with	possibly
break the habit	keep up with	regularly
generally	made no difference	so far

1. His fake ID said he was twenty-one, but he was _____ eighteen.

2. _____ and cry—it's perfectly normal.

3. Jeff visits his grandparents _____.

4. Unfortunately, the treatment _____.

5. Our plane leaves in fifteen minutes—will we _____?

6. You can't _____ work eighty hours a week!

7. _____, no one has proven him wrong.

8. If you miss a lot of school, you won't be able to _____ the class.

9. The average Australian will live a long life, and the average Japanese will _____.

10. *A battery of tests* means "a set of tests," such as medical tests. *Battery* in this phrase _____ the kind of batteries that provide electricity.

EXPANDING VOCABULARY

Transitive and Intransitive Verbs

Some verbs are **transitive**. After a transitive verb, there is a direct object, usually a noun or pronoun. For example, the verb *take* is transitive and needs a direct object: *He took **a pill**./He took **it**.* (We cannot say *He took*.)

Other verbs are **intransitive**, such as *sleep*. There can be no direct object after *sleep*: *He slept.* (We cannot say *He slept the baby*.)

Some verbs can be used either way—with or without a direct object: *I **drove my car** to the beach* or *I **drove** to the beach.*

 A Underline the verbs in the sentences below. Circle any direct objects after the verbs. Which verbs are transitive, and which are intransitive? Check (✔) your answers.

	Transitive	Intransitive
1. a. Your heart <u>beats</u> faster when you run.	☐	✔
b. Our team <u>beat</u> (theirs).	✔	☐
2. a. Please don't chew with your mouth open.	☐	☐
b. Chew your food well.	☐	☐
3. a. They treated ten people for various injuries.	☐	☐
b. Don't treat me like a child.	☐	☐
4. a. Traffic is flowing well.	☐	☐
b. Rivers flow to the sea.	☐	☐
5. a. Computers have replaced typewriters.	☐	☐
b. We'll never be able to replace you!	☐	☐
6. a. Fill in your name and address on the form.	☐	☐
b. Ms. Green is out sick, so I'm filling in.	☐	☐

B On a piece of paper, write sentences with at least six of the verbs targeted in Unit 2. Mark each verb *T* for transitive or *I* for intransitive.

A PUZZLE

There are 12 target words from Unit 2 in this puzzle. The words go across (→) and down (↓). Find the words and circle them. Then use them to complete the sentences below. (Note: The words in the sentences are not in the same order as the words in the puzzle.)

T	X	Q	Z	F	O	R	E	V	E	R
H	Z	I	N	J	U	R	I	E	S	X
E	F	A	K	E	X	L	S	V	Z	W
R	W	J	Z	B	K	I	I	X	J	I
E	X	I	S	T	S	Q	T	Z	W	T
F	Z	K	X	K	Q	U	U	V	H	H
O	M	A	T	E	R	I	A	L	X	I
R	X	B	Z	Y	W	D	T	P	Z	N
E	H	X	P	K	Z	S	I	J	V	M
T	H	R	O	U	G	H	O	U	T	X
W	V	Z	B	E	Y	O	N	D	K	B

Across

1. The baby slept _____ the trip.
2. I'll love you _____.
3. We all agree that the problem _____.
4. Luckily, their _____ weren't serious.
5. What _____ is the jacket made of?
6. We can't let the party go on _____ midnight.
7. I can't tell if it's real or _____.

Down

1. Water and oil are _____.
2. He couldn't prove it. _____, no one believed him.
3. What would you do if you were in my _____?
4. He lives _____ a mile of his job.
5. She's a _____ member of the team.

BUILDING DICTIONARY SKILLS

Understanding Codes in the Dictionary

Dictionaries use **codes** to give grammatical information about words. The codes shown here come from the *Longman Dictionary of American English* (fourth edition):

[C] = count noun (generally with both a singular and plural form: *a book/two books, one child/many children*)

[U] = uncountable or noncount noun (one form only: *bread, furniture*)

[T] = transitive verb (followed by a direct object: *buy something, love someone*)

[I] = intransitive verb (does not take a direct object: *He's sleeping. Don't fall!*)

 A   Circle the codes in this dictionary entry for the noun *demand*, and read the definitions and examples.

> **de•mand**¹ /dɪ'mænd/ *n* **1** [singular, U] the desire that people have for particular goods or services: *There isn't any* **demand for** *leaded gas anymore.* I *Nurses are in great* **demand** (=wanted by a lot of people) *these days.* **2** [C] a strong request that shows you believe you have the right to get what you ask for: *Union members will strike until the company agrees to their demands.* **3 demands** [plural] the difficult or annoying things that you need to do: *women dealing with* **the demands of** *family and career* I *The school makes heavy* **demands on** *its teachers.*

 B   Look up these nouns in your dictionary. Check (✔) the way or ways you can use each one.

1. **strength**   ☐ in the singular   ☐ in the plural   ☐ as a noncount noun

2. **operation**   ☐ in the singular   ☐ in the plural   ☐ as a noncount noun

3. **limit**   ☐ in the singular   ☐ in the plural   ☐ as a noncount noun

C Circle the codes in this dictionary entry for the verb *blink*, and read the definitions and examples.

> **blink**[1] /blɪŋk/ *v* **1** [I,T] to close and open your eyes quickly: *He blinked as he stepped out into the sunlight.* **2** [I] if a light blinks, it goes on and off continuously: *The answering machine light was blinking.*

D Look up these verbs in your dictionary. Check (✔) the way or ways you can use each one.

1. blow ☐ with a direct object following the verb ☐ with no direct object

2. prove ☐ with a direct object following the verb ☐ with no direct object

3. differ ☐ with a direct object following the verb ☐ with no direct object

Circle the letter of the word or phrase that best completes each sentence.

Example:

Some farmers do not use dangerous _____ to control insects in their fields.

a. clients   b. profits   (c.) chemicals   d. markets

1. Consumers are people who buy _____ and services.

   a. liquids   b. goods   c. advertising   d. treatment

2. What _____ him to work so hard?

   a. earned   b. gained   c. beat   d. drove

3. We figured out a _____ way to divide up the work, so everyone was happy.

   a. further   b. huge   c. fair   d. recent

4. The boy's parents let him play outside _____ he promises to stay close to home.

   a. as long as   b. therefore   c. in charge of   d. besides

5. Cats are hard to train. It is not in their _____ to try to please their trainer.

   a. quality   b. operation   c. nature   d. strength

6. It was an accident—I didn't _____ to do it.

   a. believe in   b. prove   c. mean   d. appear

7. I couldn't hear the message clearly, but it _____ the weather.

   a. kept up with   b. had something to do with   c. made a living at   d. turned something into

8. Bob drinks too much soda and wants to drink less, but it's hard to
   _____.
     a. break the   **b.** sign up   **c.** go ahead   **d.** make a
        habit   difference

9. Some jobs may not sound like fun, but they _____ are.
     a. forever   **b.** quite   **c.** as well   **d.** actually

10. All children should have the _____ to a good education.
      a. volunteer   **b.** right   **c.** lifestyle   **d.** community

11. If we want to learn the game, Robin is _____ to teach us.
      a. normal   **b.** uncertain   **c.** willing   **d.** similar

12. We wanted to go to the party, but we couldn't _____.
      a. make it   **b.** fill in   **c.** set up   **d.** take over

13. I know energy from the sun can be turned into electricity, but I don't
    understand the _____.
      a. service   **b.** percentage   **c.** process   **d.** surface

14. You have to know some history to understand the present _____.
      a. engineer   **b.** screen   **c.** injury   **d.** situation

15. Some people leave work early to _____ the heavy traffic.
      a. design   **b.** avoid   **c.** bake   **d.** blink

16. Dina wants to buy a car, but she has no _____ car in mind.
      a. particular   **b.** mental   **c.** key   **d.** economic

17. We have set up a committee and met twice _____.
      a. in return   **b.** generally   **c.** within   **d.** so far

18. Do you agree with Roberto's _____ of the problem?
      a. risk   **b.** material   **c.** chest   **d.** view

19. The team shirts are nothing special, just _____ white T-shirts with
    red numbers.
      a. artificial   **b.** plain   **c.** major   **d.** political

20. Their stores first appeared in the bigger cities but soon _____ throughout the country.

    a. announced   **b.** replaced   **c.** spread   **d.** limited

21. The school _____ children with a good hot lunch.

    a. hires   **b.** provides   **c.** blows   **d.** deals with

22. Sarah is such a wonderful painter that there is great _____ for her work.

    a. demand   **b.** condition   **c.** consumer   **d.** committee

23. If Gail doesn't study, she's _____ to fail the test.

    a. likely   **b.** developing   **c.** fake   **d.** emotional

24. The artificial flowers were _____ to her hat with a long pin.

    a. traded   **b.** chewed   **c.** attached   **d.** flowed

25. All professionals should keep up with new research and _____ in their fields.

    a. security   **b.** qualities   **c.** batteries   **d.** developments

26. Police cars _____ the road.

    a. are coming   **b.** are   **c.** are getting   **d.** are blocking
       up with   employing   rid of

27. Paul works long hours but still manages to see his friends _____.

    a. possibly   **b.** regularly   **c.** throughout **d.** beyond

28. Animals that are extinct have all died off and no longer _____.

    a. exist   **b.** treat   **c.** differ   **d.** invest

See the Answer Key on page 265.

UNIT
3

EXPLORING TECHNOLOGY

A History of Telling Time

An atomic clock from the National Institute of Standards and Technology in the United States

GETTING READY TO READ

Talk with the whole class.

1. How many people in the class wear watches? What other ways are there to find out the time?

2. How many times a day do you look to see what time it is? What is the average for the class?

   a. 0–5   **b.** 5–10   **c.** more than 10

3. Do you agree with either of these ideas? Explain.

   a. Life without clocks would be beautiful.

   b. Life without clocks would be terrible.

Look at the pictures, words, and definitions next to the reading. Then read without stopping. Don't worry about new words. Don't stop to use a dictionary. Just keep reading!

A History of Telling Time

1   No one knows when people first thought about **measuring** time. We do know that they measured it by the sun, moon, and stars, and that they first divided time into months, seasons, and years. Later, they began dividing the day into parts, like hours and minutes, and they developed simple **technology** to help them do this. Today, we have much more advanced ways to tell time, such as the atomic clock pictured on page 108, and we can measure even tiny parts of a second. A great many things have changed in how people tell time—but not everything.

2   The Sumerians, who lived in the area of present-day Iraq, were the first to divide the day into parts. Then, five or six thousand years ago, people in North Africa and the Middle East developed ways to tell the time of day. They needed some kind of clock because they now had organized religious and social activities to **attend**. That meant people needed to plan their days and set times for these **events**.

3   Among the first clocks were Egyptian obelisks.[1] The Egyptians used the movement of an obelisk's **shadow** to divide the day into morning and afternoon. Later, they placed stones on the ground around the obelisk to mark **equal** periods of time during the day, the way that numbers do on the face of a clock. That worked **fairly** well, but people could not carry obelisks with them. They needed something **portable**. So the Egyptians invented a kind of sundial[2] that is now called a shadow clock. It came into use about 3,500 years ago, around 1500 BCE.[3]

4   There were many types of sundials in Egypt and in other areas around the Mediterranean Sea. All of them, of course, depended on the sun, which was no help in telling time at night. Among the first clocks that did not depend on the sun were water clocks. There were various types of these, too. Some were designed so that water would **drip** at a **constant** rate from a tiny hole in the bottom of a **container**. Others were designed to have a container slowly

[1] an *obelisk*

[2] one kind of *sundial*

[3] *BCE* = Before the Common Era (also written *BC*, "before Christ")

(continued)

fill with water, again at a constant rate. It took a certain amount of time for the container to fill up or empty out. However, the flow of water was hard to control, so these clocks were not very **accurate**, and people still did not have a clock they could put in their pocket. Hourglasses[4] filled with sand had similar problems.

[4] an *hourglass*

5   In the early 1300s, the first mechanical clocks—machines that measured and told the time—appeared in public buildings in Italy. Around 1500, a German inventor, Peter Henlein, invented a mechanical clock that was powered by a spring.[5] Now clocks were getting smaller and easier to carry, but they still were not very accurate. Then in 1656, the Dutch scientist Christiaan Huygens invented a clock that was a big step forward. This was the first pendulum clock.[6] A pendulum moves from side to side, again and again, at a constant rate. Counting the movements of a pendulum was a better way to keep time. Huygens's first pendulum clock was accurate to within one minute a day.

[5] two *springs*

6   Developments in clock technology continued as the demand for clocks increased. Clocks were needed for factories, banking, communications, and **transportation**. Today, much of **modern** life happens at high speed and depends on having the exact time. We must also have international agreement on what the exact time is.

[6] A grandfather clock is an example of a *pendulum clock*.

7   Now we have atomic clocks, and the best of these are accurate to about one-tenth of a nanosecond[7] a day. But even with these **high-tech** clocks, we still measure a year by the time it takes the earth to go around the sun, just as people did long, long ago.

[7] a *nanosecond* = 1/1,000,000,000 (one-billionth) of a second

8   We say that it takes the earth 365 days for a trip around the sun, but that is not exactly true. A year is actually a little longer—365.242 days (or 365 days and almost six hours). So we generally add a day, February 29, every fourth year, and we call those years *leap years*. However, this creates another problem. The extra hours in four years actually add up to less than one day, so adding a day every fourth year would give us too many days. Therefore, when a year ends in -00 (for example, 1800, 1900, or 2000), we do not always make it a leap year. We do it only when we can divide the year by 4, as in 1600 and 2000. Remember that when you set your watch for the year 2100!

Quick Comprehension Check

Read these sentences. Circle T (true) or F (false).

1. People first measured time by the sun, moon, and stars.   T   F

2. People invented ways to tell time so they would know
   when to meet.   T   F

3. Water clocks depended on the sun.   T   F

4. Knowing the exact time is more important today than
   it was long ago.   T   F

5. Clocks have not changed much in the last 200 years.   T   F

6. The earth takes exactly 365 days to circle the sun.   T   F

EXPLORING VOCABULARY

Thinking about the Target Vocabulary

A   **Find the five nouns, three verbs, and six adjectives in bold in "A History of Telling Time." Add them to the chart. Write them in the order they appear in the reading. Use the singular form of any plural noun. Use the base form of each verb.**

	Nouns	Verbs	Adjectives	Other
1		*		
2				
3				
				fairly

Measuring in paragraph 1 is a gerund. A gerund is the *-ing* form of a verb used as a noun, as in
***Dancing** is fun* and *He's interested in **learning** Arabic*.

	Nouns	Verbs	Adjectives	Other
4				
6				
7				

B   **Which words are new to you? Circle them in the chart. Then find them in the reading. Look at the context. Can you guess the meaning?**

Using the Target Vocabulary

A   **These sentences are about the reading. Complete them with the words in the box.**

constant	events	modern	technology
dripped	fairly	shadow	transportation

1. Thousands of years ago, people began developing _____ for telling time. Here, the word refers to simple tools, skills, and materials. (It can also mean "advanced machines and ways of doing things based on science and the use of computers.")

2. People needed to tell time when they began to have organized activities happening at particular times and places. These activities included religious and social _____.

3. The Egyptians were the first to tell time by the movement of an obelisk's _____ (a darker area made by blocking sunlight).

4. Using an obelisk to tell time worked _____ well. It wasn't great, but it was better than nothing.

5. Some water clocks were designed so that water _____, or fell little by little, from a tiny hole.

6. Water would drip out of a water clock at a _____ rate. It never speeded up or slowed down.

7. The phrase _____ *life* refers to the way people live now or have lived in recent times.

8. The demand for clocks increased because of modern communications and _____ (the process of taking people and goods from one place to another, by air, land, or sea).

B These sentences are also **about the reading**. What is the meaning of each **boldfaced** word? Circle a, b, or c.

1. We use clocks to **measure** time. *Measure something* means
   a. use and enjoy it.
   b. find out the size or amount of it.
   c. keep up with it.

2. If people want to **attend** an event, they have to know what time to be there. *Attend an event* means to
   a. replace it.
   b. be present for it.
   c. organize it.

3. The stones on the ground around an obelisk marked **equal** periods of time. *Equal* means
   a. daylight.
   b. short.
   c. the same.

4. Obelisks were not **portable**. *Portable* means
   a. able to be carried.
   b. nice to look at.
   c. in great demand.

5. A water clock had to have a **container**. A container is
   a. a designer or engineer.
   b. a process.
   c. something that can be filled.

6. Water clocks and hourglasses were not very **accurate**. We call a clock *accurate* when it
   a. costs very little.
   b. measures time exactly.
   c. can be carried easily.

7. Today, we have **high-tech** clocks, like atomic clocks. *High-tech* means
   a. fairly accurate.
   b. beautifully designed.
   c. using advanced technology.

DEVELOPING READING SKILLS

Text Organization

 A **How is the reading "A History of Telling Time" organized?**

☐ **1.** The writer compares and contrasts ways that different cultures measure time.

☐ **2.** The writer describes developments in measuring time in chronological order.

☐ **3.** The writer presents arguments for and against the idea of measuring time.

B **Scan the reading for information on these topics. Number them in order from 1 (the earliest development) to 8 (the most recent).**

_____ Countries around the world had to agree on the exact time.

_____ People measured time by the sun, moon, and stars.

_____ Peter Henlein invented a spring-powered clock.

_____ The Egyptian shadow clock, the first portable clock, was invented.

_____ People used hourglasses.

_____ Christiaan Huygens invented a pendulum clock.

_____ The first mechanical clocks appeared in public buildings in Italy.

_____ The Egyptians built obelisks to help them tell time.

Scanning

Read these statements about the reading. Scan the reading for the information you need to complete them.

1. People in _____ and _____ were the first to develop ways to tell the time of day.

2. People started needing clocks and setting times to meet after they developed _____ and _____.

3. Obelisks and _____ depended on the sun.

4. A _____ measured time by filling up a container with water, or emptying one out, at a constant rate.

5. The first really accurate clock was a _____ clock, invented in the year _____.

6. The best atomic clocks are accurate to _____.

7. It takes _____ days and _____ hours for the earth to circle the sun.

8. A year with 366 days is called a _____.

Understanding Reference Words

Remember: A **reference word** takes the place of a noun or a noun phrase. It refers back to someone or something already named.

Pronouns, such as *he*, *she*, *it*, and *them*, are reference words. The words *one*, *ones*, *this*, *that*, *these*, and *those* can also be reference words.

What do the boldfaced reference words mean in these sentences? Look back at the reading. Write your answers on the lines.

1. Paragraph 2: **They** needed some kind of clock . . . _____

_____

2. Paragraph 2: . . . and set times for **these events**. _____

_____

3. Paragraph 4: All of **them**, of course, depended . . . _____

_____

4. Paragraph 8: However, **this** creates another problem. _____

_____

5. Paragraph 8: We **do it** only when . . . _____

_____

EXPANDING VOCABULARY

New Contexts

A Complete the sentences with the target words in the box. There are two extra words.

| accurate | dripping | fairly | measuring | portable |
| constant | equal | high-tech | modern | technology |

1. I have an old _____ radio that I take to the beach.
2. Her Spanish isn't perfect, but she speaks it _____ well.
3. The course is on _____ Chinese history, the last 75 years.
4. You won't believe all the things his new phone can do. It is very _____.
5. Hannah is _____ the flour for a cake she's making.
6. He is studying computer _____. He wants to be an engineer.
7. I do the same work he does, so we should get _____ pay.
8. The shower in the upstairs bathroom won't stop _____.

B These sentences also use the target words **in new contexts**. Complete them with the words in the box. There are three extra words.

| accurate | constant | equal | high-tech | shadows |
| attend | containers | events | portable | transportation |

1. Tickets for professional sports _____ have become very expensive.
2. I drove the whole way there at a _____ speed of 55 miles per hour.
3. We try to buy food in _____ that we can re-use.
4. He gave the police an _____ report of the accident.
5. Are there _____ numbers of students in the three classes?
6. The law says children must _____ school regularly.
7. _____ grow longer late in the day.

Building on the Vocabulary: Word Grammar

> The **root** of the words *portable* and *transportation* is *port*. It comes from a Latin word meaning "carry." Something that is portable is something you can carry. *Transportation* refers to the process or business of carrying people and goods to other places. The verb form is *transport*: *We transported the computers by truck.*

Choose your own ways to complete the following sentences.

1. The first _____ were not portable, but now people can buy portable ones.
2. Modern transportation includes _____, _____, and _____.
3. In my country, businesses often transport goods by _____.

Using New Words

Work with a partner. Choose five target words from the chart on pages 111–112. On a piece of paper, use each word in a sentence.

PUTTING IT ALL TOGETHER

Discussion

Talk about these questions in a small group.

1. How did people tell time before the first mechanical clocks were invented? Name three or more ways.
2. When is it important to be on time? How important is it? If a friend is supposed to meet you, but he or she is late, how long are you likely to wait?
3. Although we need international agreement on what time it is, not everyone marks time by the same calendar. What examples can you list of calendars used by various cultures? What do you know about each one?

Writing

Choose a topic. Write a paragraph.

1. There are many popular sayings about time in English— for example, "Time is money" and "Time flies when you're having fun." Give your opinion of one of these sayings, or explain a saying from your first language that refers to time.

2. Write about question 2 from **Discussion** on page 117.

CHAPTER 10

Out with the Old, In with the New?

The art of Chinese writing

GETTING READY TO READ

Read the questions. Check (✔) your answers. Then find out how your classmates answered the questions, and write the numbers in the chart.

Questions	Class Survey Results
1. Did you use a calculator[1] in school when you were young? ☐ Yes ☐ No	_____ out of _____ people used calculators.
2. Did you spend much time in school practicing your handwriting when you were a child? ☐ Yes ☐ No	_____ out of _____ people worked hard on their handwriting.
3. Which statement is most true for you? ☐ I prefer to write by hand. ☐ I prefer to write on a computer.	_____ by hand _____ on a computer

[1] *a calculator*

119

READING

Look at the picture, words, and definitions next to the reading. Then read without stopping.

Out with the Old, In with the New?

1   Modern technology is causing changes in our lives that have some people worried. Everyone agrees that new inventions have made life easier, but perhaps we need to ask, "Are we losing something along the way?"

2   Jack Riley is a fifth-grade student in Vancouver, Canada, and he is **annoyed**. His teacher has just said, "No more calculators in math class." Jack likes using a calculator to add, **subtract**, **multiply**, or divide, but his teacher is worried about her students' basic math skills. She wants them doing more math in their heads and on paper. She recently read about a study on the math skills of Canadian college students. Some of the students had lived and studied all their lives in Canada, while others had come to Canada from schools in China. The researchers found that the Chinese students were quicker at doing simple math problems and far better at doing **complex** ones. They also learned that the Chinese students had used calculators much less often during their early school years than the Canadians had. Jack's teacher has also read the results of a study showing that Canadian students are not keeping up in math with students from Japan, Korea, Singapore, or England. Jack's teacher **blames** technology.

3   Kate Gladstone of Albany, New York, has similar feelings about technology. Gladstone is "the Handwriting Repairwoman." She helps people **improve** their handwriting so others can read it better—and sometimes so they can read it themselves. Businesses have asked her to work with their employees, and many doctors have taken her courses. People in the United States often **make fun of** doctors' bad handwriting, but Gladstone says it is nothing to laugh about. "We've got to be aware that handwriting is important," she says. Doctors have to write clear prescriptions[1] because their patients' lives may depend on them. Most of us have to be able to write notes to co-workers,[2] **fill out** forms, and write addresses that the post office can read. Gladstone says that too many people never learned to write clearly in school, and too many people think it does not **matter** anymore. She feels that in the age of computers, handwriting is not getting the attention it **deserves**.

[1] a *prescription* = a doctor's written order for a particular medicine for a sick person

[2] *co-workers* = people who work together

4   Li You lives in the city of Yangshuo in Guangxi, China. He writes every day on a computer, using a Chinese word processing[3] program. Soon after he began doing this, his memory for writing Chinese characters[4] by hand began to fail. He would pick up a pen and be unable to write something that he had learned as a child. Many of his friends have had the same problem. They used to be able to write thousands of characters. Now they joke about how often they try to write a character but cannot remember how. Li does 95 percent of his writing at the computer now and says, "I can go for a month without picking up a pen," so he is not worried. However, some people have a different view of the situation. "A long time ago, we all wrote much better," says Ye Zi, who works with Li. "It's a cultural **loss**."

5   Are computers and calculators **robbing** people of **valuable** skills? Some people think so. Others say such questions just show that some of us cannot deal with change.

6   Jack's teacher thinks that students lose something when they depend on calculators, but other math teachers disagree. Kate Gladstone talks about the importance of handwriting, but she uses e-mail, too. Among writers of Chinese, opinions **vary** on the old way versus[5] the new. Some remember that until the 1900s, the brush—not the pen—was the traditional tool for writing Chinese, and writing was something that few people knew how to do. The pen replaced the brush because it was easier to use and carry around. Many people did not like this new development, but as the pen became more popular, it helped more people learn to write.

7   We cannot avoid change, says Ming Zhou, a Microsoft researcher in Beijing. "It's just the way it is." He says the modern way is always to do things faster. "When culture and speed come into **conflict**, speed wins."

[3] *word processing =* the use of a computer and certain software to write

[4] the Chinese *character* for "life"

[5] *versus =* (also *vs.*) as compared with, as opposed to

Kate Gladstone was quoted in "Why Farhad Can't Write" by Farhad Manjoo, retrieved May 24, 2009 from http://www.wired.com, culture/lifestyle/news/2000/08/38139. Li You, Ye Zi, and Ming Zhou were quoted in "In China, Computer Use Erodes Traditional Handwriting, Stirring a Cultural Debate" by Jennifer Lee, retrieved May 24, 2009 from http://www.nytimes.com/2001/02/01/technology/01LOST.html.

Quick Comprehension Check

Read these sentences. Circle T (true) or F (false).

1. All the people described in the reading feel the same way about technology.   T   F

2. Some people think the use of calculators hurts children's math skills.   T   F

3. A study was done in Canada on the math skills of college students.   T   F

4. According to the reading, handwriting does not matter anymore.   T   F

5. Some writers in China are forgetting how to write Chinese characters with a pen.   T   F

6. Some people worry about losing the old ways, and some do not.   T   F

EXPLORING VOCABULARY

Thinking about the Target Vocabulary

 Find the two nouns, ten verbs, and three adjectives in **bold** in "Out with the Old, In with the New?" Add them to the chart. Use the base form of each verb.

	Nouns	Verbs	Adjectives	Other
2				

	Nouns	Verbs	Adjectives	Other
3				
4				
5				
6				
7				

B Which words or phrases are new to you? Circle them in the chart. Then find them in the reading. Look at the context. Can you guess the meaning?

Using the Target Vocabulary

A These sentences are **about the reading**. Complete them with the words in the box.

annoyed	complex	multiply	valuable
blames	loss	robs	vary

1. Jack Riley is a little angry with his teacher. He is _____ about her new rule.
2. Jack likes using a calculator when he has to _____ one number by another, as in 45 × 32.
3. The Chinese students in the study were better than the Canadians at doing _____ math problems. These were difficult problems with many parts or steps.
4. Jack's teacher thinks technology is responsible for the Canadian students' poor scores on math tests. She _____ technology.

5. Ye Zi believes that the Chinese culture loses something when people forget how to write characters. "It's a cultural _____."

6. Are computers and calculators taking something away from us? Some people think technology _____ people of useful skills.

7. Some skills are worth a lot. They are _____.

8. Not all writers of Chinese have the same opinion. Opinions _____ from one person to the next.

B   These sentences are also **about the reading**. Complete them with the words and phrases in the box.

conflict	fill out	make fun of	subtract
deserves	improve	matter	

1. Jack likes using a calculator to _____ one number from another, as in 83 – 69.

2. Some people want to make their handwriting better. Kate Gladstone can help them _____ it.

3. People in the United States often joke that no one can read doctors' handwriting. They _____ doctors' handwriting.

4. Clear handwriting is important if you have to _____ a form, such as a job application.

5. Kate Gladstone says many people believe good handwriting is no longer important. They think it doesn't _____.

6. She thinks handwriting should get more attention in school. It _____ more attention, she says.

7. Culture and speed have come into _____, a situation in which people have to choose between opposing sides.

DEVELOPING READING SKILLS

Comparing and Contrasting

Use information from the reading to complete each diagram below. What do the people have in common? How do they differ?

1. The Canadian study:

The first group	Both groups	The second group

- grew up in ___Canada___

- used _____

_____

- go to college in Canada

- can do math

- grew up in _____

- _____

_____

- _____

_____

2. Li You and Ye Zi:

Li You	Both	Ye Zi

- thinks _____

_____

_____

- live in China
- can _____
- can _____

- thinks _____

_____

_____

Understanding Inference

Sometimes the answers to questions about a reading are not directly stated in the reading. You cannot scan it to find the answers. You must put ideas from the reading together with what you already know. You must make **inferences**.

These are inference questions. The answers are not given in the reading, but you can answer the questions if you understand the reading. Write your answers on a piece of paper.

1. What does Jack's teacher believe about calculators?
2. What does Kate Gladstone want schools to do?
3. What would Ye Zi probably want his children to learn in school?

Summarizing

On a piece of paper, write a summary of the reading. Include the answers to these questions. (Write 1–2 sentences for each). If you wish, you can begin:

According to "Out with the Old, In with the New?" some people worry that . . .

- What does the reading say some people worry about?
- What are two examples from the reading of technological advances and their negative effects?
- What two different opinions about change does the writer describe?

EXPANDING VOCABULARY

New Contexts

A Complete the sentences with the target words and phrases in the box. There are two extra words.

annoyed	conflict	losses	robbed
blame	fill out	make fun of	valuable
complex	improved	mattered	vary

1. Because he is the slowest runner, the other boys laugh at him and _____ him.

2. You have to _____ this application if you want to rent a car.

3. The team has a record of six wins, no _____, and one tie.

4. I was _____ with my brother for not giving me the message.

5. Can the police prove that he is the one who _____ the store?

6. Do you understand the political situation? It's fairly _____.

7. We hope the _____ between the two nations does not develop into a war.

8. Schools across the state _____ in what and how they teach.

9. When the artist became famous, his paintings became more _____.

10. His parents _____ him for the broken window, but it was actually his sister who did it.

Read these sentences. Write the boldfaced target words next to their definitions. There is one extra definition. Put an X next to it.

a. When you **subtract** 20 from 30, you get 10.

b. When you **multiply** 20 times 30, you get 600.

c. You can **improve** your skills with practice.

d. Two people doing equal work **deserve** equal pay.

e. Does it **matter** who goes first?

Target Words or Phrases   **Definitions**

1. _____ = make something better

2. _____ = be important, have an effect on what happens

3. _____ = add a number to itself a particular number of times

4. _____ = take a number or an amount from another number or amount

5. _____ = should get something (because they have earned it)

6. _____ = figure out how many times one number contains another (usually smaller) number

Building on the Vocabulary: Word Grammar

The verb *rob* and the verb *steal* have similar meanings, but they are used differently.

- Someone robs a person or a company: *He robbed a bank.*
- Someone steals a thing (from a person or company): *He stole money from the bank.*

Write two sentences. Use *rob* and *steal*.

1. _____

2. _____

Using New Words

Work with a partner. Choose five target words or phrases from the chart on pages 122–123. On a piece of paper, use each word or phrase in a sentence.

PUTTING IT ALL TOGETHER

Sharing Opinions

Talk about the following opinions in a small group. Tell why you agree or disagree.

Opinion 1	Children need to spend a lot of time in school developing good handwriting.
Opinion 2	Children should spend more school time learning to write on a computer than learning to write by hand.
Opinion 3	Children should not waste school time practicing handwriting or typing at a computer keyboard. In the future, we will speak to computers and they will do our writing for us.

Writing

Choose a topic. Write a paragraph.

1. Think of a tradition that has changed in your country in recent years. Describe the change and give your opinion of it.

2. Some people love new technology, others aren't interested in it, and some are afraid of it. What about you? What is your relationship with modern technology? Give an example from your life.

CHAPTER 11

Appropriate Technologies

Keeping vegetables fresh in a cooler made from two clay pots with wet sand in between*

GETTING READY TO READ

Talk with a partner or in a small group.

1. What percentage of the people in the world do you think have no electricity?

   a. less than 10%   **b.** about 18%   **c.** about 33%

2. Do you know the phrases *developed countries* and *developing countries*? Read the definitions and list some examples of each.

   developed countries = rich countries with many industries, comfortable living for most people, and (usually) governments chosen by the people

   Examples: _____

   developing countries = poor countries without much industry that are working to improve their people's lives

   Examples: _____

* Developed by Mohammed Bah Abba of Nigeria for use in hot, dry places with no electricity

READING

Look at the pictures, words, and definitions next to the reading. Then read without stopping.

Appropriate Technologies

1   You are probably reading this book in a developed country. So when you hear the word *technology*, you are likely to think of computers, high-tech phones, cars, and so on. Those of us who live in such countries can look forward to new and better **models** of all these things each year. Modern technology has made life in developed countries much easier for us. Technology can make life easier in developing countries, too, but it has to be technology of another kind because the needs in such countries are very different. About two billion people—one-third of the people on earth—do not even have electricity. What they need is technology that is **appropriate** for their situations. That is, they need technology that will help them meet basic needs for food, water, clothes, housing, health services, and ways to make a living.

2   The term *appropriate technologies* means types of technology that
   - use materials available in the local area;
   - can be understood, built, and **repaired** by the people who use them;
   - bring communities together to **solve** local problems.

3   Some appropriate technologies are beautifully simple. For example, a project in Sri Lanka is using sunlight to make drinking water safe. Clear bottles are filled with water and placed in the sun for six hours. That is usually enough time for the sun to heat the water and kill germs.[1] If the weather is cool or cloudy, it takes two days. This **method** has been proven to help people stay healthier.

4   Amy Smith is an inventor with a passion[2] for designing appropriate technologies. Smith studied engineering at MIT, the Massachusetts Institute of Technology (in the United States), and then spent four years in Botswana (in Africa). She taught math, science, and English there, and she trained farmers to take care of bees so they could get honey[3] from them. In Botswana, she realized that she could help people more by using her skills as an engineer. Smith said, "The longer I was there, the more I realized there were **plenty** of inventions that could improve the quality of life."

(continued)

[1] *germs* = very small living things that can make a person sick

[2] a *passion* = a strong love

[3] Bees produce *honey*.

5   So Smith went back to MIT and started working on low-tech inventions. Her first great invention was a screenless hammermill. A hammermill is a machine that grinds[4] **grain** into flour. Usually a hammermill needs a **screen** to separate the flour from the unwanted parts of the grain. But screens often break, and they are hard to replace, so regular hammermills are not much use in **rural** Africa. Women there often end up grinding grain by hand and spending hours each day to do it. Smith's invention does not need a screen. It is cheap to build, simple to use, easy to repair, and it does not need electricity. With this machine, a woman can grind as much grain in a minute as she used to do in an hour.

[4] *grinds* = crushes between two hard, moving surfaces

6   Smith's invention has been a great success in Africa, but some other good ideas have not done so well. In northern Ghana, another project designed to help women failed partly for cultural reasons. The women in this area do most of the farming, and they spend a lot of time and energy walking to and from their farms. Most of the time, they are carrying heavy **loads** on their heads. They are very much in need of a better way to transport farm products, tools, water, and so on. Because bicycles are popular in the region, a bicycle trailer seemed to be a good **solution** to the problem. The trailer was like a shopping cart[5] but had two wheels and was attached to the back of a bike. However, the idea did not work. For one thing, it is the men in northern Ghana, not the women, who own and ride bicycles. In addition, the type of bicycle offered to the women was a bicycle with a crossbar.[6] A woman wearing a dress, as is traditional there, cannot ride such a bicycle.

[5] a *shopping cart*

[6] a bicycle with a *crossbar*

7   Amy Smith and others are trying to develop technologies that do not need electricity. However, developing countries would **be better off** if they had it. Electricity would improve education and communication, let doctors store medicines that must stay cold, and do much more. The **production** of electricity sometimes causes **pollution**, but creative engineers can find ways to produce it without destroying **the environment**, perhaps by using energy from the sun, wind, or water. Of course, the problems of developing nations cannot all be solved by thinkers like Amy Smith, but many can. As she says, "Technology isn't the only solution, but it can certainly be part of the solution."

Amy Smith was quoted in "MIT Grad Student Designs Low-Cost Solution for High-Tech African Problem" by Denise Brehm, November 29, 1999, retrieved May 24, 2009, from http://web.mit.edu/newsoffice.

Quick Comprehension Check

Read these sentences. Circle T (true) or F (false).

1. Few people in the world are without electricity. T F

2. The same technology will not work everywhere. T F

3. *Appropriate technologies* means the most modern, high-tech machines. T F

4. Amy Smith is an engineer and an inventor. T F

5. Culture can influence how people use or feel about new technology. T F

6. Electricity would not help developing countries. T F

EXPLORING VOCABULARY

Thinking about the Target Vocabulary

A Find the ten nouns, three verbs, and two adjectives in **bold** in "Appropriate Technologies." Add them to the chart. Use the singular form of any plural noun. Use the base form of each verb.

	Nouns	Verbs	Adjectives	Other
1				
2				
3				
4				
5				
6				

	Nouns	Verbs	Adjectives	Other
7				
*				

* Include the article *the*.

 B   Which words and phrases are new to you? Circle them here. Then find them in the reading. Look at the context. Can you guess the meaning?

Using the Target Vocabulary

 A   These sentences are **about the reading**. What is the meaning of each **boldfaced** word or phrase? Circle a, b, or c.

1. Each year, carmakers produce new **models** of cars. *Models* means
   a. customers.   b. habits.   c. certain types or designs.

2. Technology for use in developing countries should be easy to **repair**. *Repair* means
   a. blame.   b. fix.   c. drip.

3. When the people in a community share a problem, they need to work together to **solve** it. When you solve a problem, you
   a. find an answer to it.   b. make fun of it.   c. multiply it.

4. They have a simple **method** for making their drinking water safe. *Method* means
   a. a planned way of doing something   b. a conflict between two forces   c. a bad habit.

5. Amy Smith realized there were **plenty of** inventions that could improve the lives of Africans. If you have plenty of something, you have
   a. a small amount of it.   b. enough or more than enough of it.   c. a decreasing amount of it.

6. There is little modern technology in **rural** Africa. *Rural* means relating to

a. country areas, not the city.

b. expensive goods.

c. high-tech inventions.

7. Water power is often used in the **production** of electricity. *The production of something* means

a. the investment in it.

b. the explanation of it.

c. the process for making it.

8. Clean ways to make electricity do not hurt **the environment**. *The environment* means

a. all our land, water, and air.

b. people's lifestyles.

c. types of transportation.

B Read each definition and look at the paragraph number. Look back at the reading on pages 131–132 to find the **boldfaced** word or phrase to match the definition. Write it in the chart.

Definition	Paragraph	Target Word or Phrase
1. right for a certain purpose, situation, or time	1	
2. seeds of plants such as rice, corn, or wheat that are used for food	5	
3. a wire net (like the material used in windows to let air in and keep insects out)	5	
4. amounts of things that are carried by a person, animal, truck, etc.	6	
5. a way of solving a problem	6	
6. be richer, more comfortable, more successful	7	
7. dangerous amounts of dirt or chemicals in the air, water, etc.	7	

DEVELOPING READING SKILLS

Problem and Solution

Use information from "Appropriate Techologies" to complete the chart.

	Problem	Solution Described	Has the problem been solved?	
			Yes	No
1.	basic needs not met in developing countries	appropriate technologies		✓
2.	unsafe drinking water in Sri Lanka			
3.	long hours grinding grain in rural Africa			
4.	no transportation for farmers in Ghana			
5.	little electricity in developing nations			

Cause and Effect

Complete each sentence about the reading.

1. The technology needs of developing countries are different from those of developed nations because _____

_____.

2. People in Sri Lanka put bottles of water in the sun because _____

_____.

3. Amy Smith's screenless hammermill is a good example of an appropriate technology because _____

_____.

4. The women in Ghana did not use the bicycle trailers because

_____

_____.

Supporting Details

Write two statements with details that support each of the general statements below.

1. *Technology* means different things to people depending on where they live.

   To people in developing countries, technology means ways to meet basic needs.

   To people in developed countries, technology means high-tech inventions like computers and cars.

2. Appropriate technologies do not depend on high-tech machines or processes.

3. Bringing electricity to developing countries could have both good and bad effects.

4. Technology can make people's lives easier.

EXPANDING VOCABULARY

New Contexts

A   Complete the sentences with the target words in the box. There are two extra words.

method	plenty	production	rural	solve
models	pollution	repair	screen	the environment

1. He lives on a farm in a quiet _____ area.
2. The accident was so bad that they can't possibly _____ the car.
3. You can get a TV at SuperBuy. There are lots of _____ to choose from.
4. I like her _____ of cooking rice. It has just a few simple steps.
5. There's no need to rush—we have _____ of time.
6. He thinks money will _____ all his problems.
7. The industry had to stop using chemicals that were bad for _____.
8. Demand for the game was high, so the company increased _____.

B   These sentences also use the target words and phrases **in new contexts**. Complete them with the words and phrases in the box. There are three extra words.

appropriate	grain	model	production	screen
be better off	loads	pollution	repairs	solutions

1. Bicycles are one form of transportation that doesn't cause air _____.
2. Whole _____ breads are better for you because they use every part of the seed.

3. If there are no seats on the bus, we'd _____ waiting for the next one.

4. A _____ door won't keep out the cold.

5. It's important to wear something _____ to a job interview.

6. Students often carry heavy _____ of books in backpacks.

7. If we all work together on these problems, I'm sure we can come up with good _____.

Building on the Vocabulary: Word Grammar

> The word *technology* can be:
>
> - a noncount noun: *New technology is exciting.*
> - a count noun, often plural: *Appropriate technologies are simple to use.* When it is plural, it means "types of technology."
>
> Other nouns that are usually noncount, such as *fruit* and *cheese*, may also have a plural form meaning "types of."
>
> > Eat plenty of *fruits* and vegetables. = Eat plenty of types of fruit . . .
> >
> > My favorite *cheeses* come from France. = My favorite types of cheese . . .

Circle the plural form when the noun means "types of." Circle the noncount form when it does not.

1. Some (food / foods) will affect the brain immediately; others won't.

2. Please give the cat her (food / foods).

3. They sell a variety of (coffee / coffees) from Latin America.

4. I'll have a cup of (coffee / coffees), please.

5. I use (shampoo / shampoos) to wash my hair.

6. The supermarket has many different (shampoo / shampoos).

Using New Words

Work with a partner. Choose five target words or phrases from the chart on pages 133–134. On a piece of paper, use each word or phrase in a sentence.

PUTTING IT ALL TOGETHER

Discussion

Work with a partner or in a small group.

1. Fill in the chart with examples of modern technology that you use. Write what people had to do before the invention of each type of technology.

Modern Technology	In the Past
1. dishwashers	People washed dishes by hand.
2.	
3.	
4.	
5.	

2. Consider each of the types of technology in your chart. Which ones would you miss the most and the least if you didn't have them? Why?

3. Amy Smith spent four years living and working in a rural area of a developing country. Do you know anyone who has done something like that? Would you like to do it yourself? Why or why not?

Writing

Choose question 2 or 3 from Discussion above. Write a paragraph that answers the question.

CHAPTER 12

Technology in Science Fiction

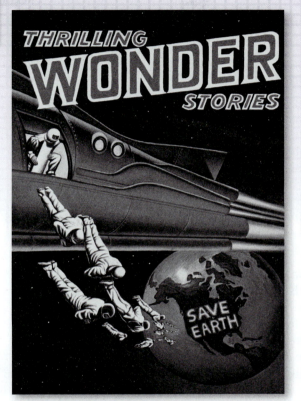

A science fiction magazine cover from 1941

Talk with a partner or in a small group.

1. *Science fiction* means stories about future developments in science and technology and their effects on people. Sometimes these stories include travel by spaceship.[1] There have been many popular science-fiction movies, such as *Star Wars*. What others can you name?

2. **a.** Look at the magazine cover above. What is happening in the picture?

   b. An artist created this magazine cover in 1941. How well did the artist imagine the future? Explain.

[1] a *spaceship*

141

Look at the pictures, words, and definitions next to the reading. Then read without stopping.

Technology in Science Fiction

1   Facts are pieces of information we can show to be true. When we read history, we want to know the facts—what really happened. Fiction is the opposite. Writers of fiction **make up** stories, telling of people and events that come from the writer's **imagination**. Science fiction writers imagine not only people and events but, perhaps most importantly, technology. They often write about the effects of that technology on a person, a group, or **society**. These writers usually set their stories in the future. Some of them have **predicted** technology that seemed impossible at the time but really does exist today.

2   An Englishwoman, Mary Shelley, was one of the first writers of science fiction. In 1818, she wrote the book *Frankenstein,* which tells the story of a young scientist, Dr. Frankenstein, who wants to create a human life. He puts together parts of dead people's bodies, including—by mistake—the brain of a **criminal**, and then uses electricity to bring the creature[1] to life. However, he cannot control the creature, and it kills him. Since then, the idea of a "mad scientist" (someone who tries to use science and technology to gain power) has been very popular in science fiction, especially in the movies.

3   In 1863, the French writer Jules Verne wrote the first of his many great science fiction **adventure** stories, *Cinq Semaines en Ballon (Five Weeks in a Balloon).* It is the story of three men traveling across Africa by hot-air balloon.[2] Readers loved it, but many were **confused**: Was it fact or fiction? The story sounded unlikely, but the writer's **style** and the **scientific** details made it seem true.

4   Later, Jules Verne wrote *Paris au Vingtième Siècle (Paris in the Twentieth Century),* a story he set in the 1960s, 100 years into the future. This story has **descriptions** of high-speed trains, gas-powered cars, calculators, skyscrapers,[3] and modern methods of communication. Verne imagined all these things at a time when **neither** he **nor** anyone in Paris had even a radio! In another book, *De la Terre à la Lune (From the Earth to the Moon),* he predicted that people would travel in **outer space** and walk on the moon, a prediction that came true on July 20, 1969. Verne even got some of the details right. Both in his book and in real life, there were three astronauts[4] making the flight to the moon, they **took off** from Florida, and they came down in the Pacific Ocean on their return.

[1] a *creature* = a living thing (but not a plant)

[2] a *hot-air balloon*

[3] a *skyscraper* = an extremely tall building

[4] an *astronaut* = someone who travels and works in outer space

5   Space travel continued to be a popular subject for science fiction in the twentieth **century**. The best writers based the science and technology in their stories on a real understanding of the science and technology of their time. Computers, robots,[5] and genetic engineering[6] all appeared in the pages of science fiction long before they appeared in the news.

[5] a *robot*

[6] *genetic engineering* = the science of changing the genes of living things

6   The following quotation comes from a story by the great science fiction writer Isaac Asimov. He wrote these words in 1954. When you read them, remember that at that time, people had no computers in their homes. In fact, the few computers that existed were as big as some people's homes. In "The Fun They Had," Asimov describes a child of the future using a personal computer to learn math:

7   Margie went into the schoolroom. It was right next to her bedroom, and the mechanical teacher was on and waiting for her. . . .

8   The screen was lit up, and it said: "Today's arithmetic lesson is on the addition of proper fractions. Please insert yesterday's homework in the proper slot."

9   Margie did so with a sigh. She was thinking about the old schools they had when her grandfather's grandfather was a little boy. All the kids from the whole neighborhood came, laughing and shouting in the schoolyard, sitting together in the schoolroom. . . .

10   And the teachers were people. . . .

11   Back in 1954, readers probably found Asimov's story hard to believe. Today, his ideas do not seem so strange, do they? Maybe we should pay more attention to what science fiction writers are saying today about the world of tomorrow. But we should also remember that their predictions have been wrong more often than right. Here we are in the twenty-first century without flying cars, vacations on the moon, or robots cooking our dinner. And **in spite of** computers, people still do go to school.

Isaac Asimov's story "The Fun They Had" appears in *The Best of Isaac Asimov* (New York: Doubleday & Company, 1974), 153–155.

Quick Comprehension Check

Read these sentences. Circle T (true) or F (false).

1. Science fiction is often about the technology of the future.   T   F

2. People began writing science fiction in the 1900s.   T   F

3. A lot of science fiction is about travel in outer space.   T   F

4. Science fiction writers have imagined technology that was later invented.   T   F

5. A writer fifty years ago imagined computers replacing schools and teachers.   T   F

6. The predictions of science fiction writers are generally correct.   T   F

EXPLORING VOCABULARY

Thinking about the Target Vocabulary

 A   Find the eight nouns, three verbs, and two adjectives in **bold** in "Technology in Science Fiction." Add them to the chart. Use the singular form of any plural nouns. Use the base form of each verb.

	Nouns	Verbs	Adjectives	Other
1				
2				
3				

	Nouns	Verbs	Adjectives	Other
4				
				neither . . . nor
5				
11				in spite of

B Which words or phrases are new to you? Circle them here. Then find them in the reading. Look at the context. Can you guess the meaning?

Using the Target Vocabulary

 A These sentences are **about the reading**. Complete them with the words and phrases in the box.

> criminal   imagination   neither . . . nor   predicted   style
> description   in spite of   outer space   scientific   took off

1. The people and events in fiction come from the writer's
   _____ (his or her ability to think of new ideas or form
   mental pictures).

2. Writers have imagined technologies of the future and described them
   in their stories. They have _____ technologies that had
   not yet been invented.

3. By mistake, Dr. Frankenstein gave his creature the brain of a
   _____, a person who broke the law and committed crimes.

4. Jules Verne's _____ of writing—or the way he told his
   stories—made them seem true.

5. Verne made readers believe his stories by including information
   about science. His stories were full of _____ details that
   sounded true.

6. Verne wrote a story in which he described Paris 100 years into the
   future. The story gave a _____ of what Paris would be like
   at that time.

7. Verne used his imagination to write about advanced technology. He didn't have any such technology. _____ he _____ anyone in Paris had even a radio, much less a phone or a car.

8. Verne predicted that people would travel into _____ and walk on the surface of the moon.

9. In both the book *From the Earth to the Moon* and in real life, the astronauts _____ from Florida. That is, their spaceships went up into the air from Florida.

10. Computers have not replaced teachers and classrooms. People still go to school _____ computers (that is, even though computers exist).

 B **These sentences are also about the reading. What is the meaning of each boldfaced word or phrase? Circle a, b, or c.**

1. Writers of history shouldn't **make things up**, but writers of science fiction always do. *Make something up* means
   a. report it.   **b.** invent it.   **c.** prove it.

2. Science fiction often deals with the effects of future technology on **society**. *Society* means
   a. the author.   **b.** machines.   **c.** people in general.

3. Jules Verne's science fiction stories are full of danger and **adventure**. *Adventure* means
   a. operations.   **b.** goods and services.   **c.** exciting experiences.

4. Readers of *Five Weeks in a Balloon* were **confused**. *They were confused* means they
   a. didn't know what to believe.   **b.** didn't like the book.   **c.** didn't want the story to end.

5. Science fiction books and movies were popular during the twentieth **century**. A century is
   a. a period of 100 years.   **b.** a lifetime.   **c.** a lifestyle.

DEVELOPING READING SKILLS

Paraphrasing

One sentence in each pair paraphrases the sentence from the reading. Circle the correct answer.

1. Science fiction writers imagine not only people and events but, perhaps most importantly, technology.

   a. Like other writers, science fiction writers make up stories, but a key thing they do is think of new technology.

   b. Science fiction is the most important way that we learn about people, events, and technology of the future.

2. Some of them have predicted technology that seemed impossible at the time but really does exist today.

   a. Today we have technology that was impossible even to imagine in the past.

   b. Some science fiction writers have been very good at imagining future technology.

3. The story sounded unlikely, but the writer's style and the scientific details made it seem true.

   a. Jules Verne's writing style and use of scientific details made readers wonder if his story could actually be true.

   b. Readers didn't like Jules Verne's story, but they believed it because of the style and the scientific details.

4. Here we are in the twenty-first century without flying cars, vacations on the moon, or robots cooking our dinner.

   a. Twenty-first century technology so far has been a disappointment in many ways.

   b. Many predictions that science fiction writers have made have not come true.

Using Context Clues

The paragraphs in the reading from Asimov's story "The Fun They Had" contain words you may not know. Answer these questions about the story using the context to guess word meanings.

1. On the computer screen, Margie can read these words:

   Today's arithmetic lesson is on the addition of proper fractions.

   Which words are related to math? Circle them.

2. The computer tells Margie to "insert yesterday's homework in the proper slot." A slot is a long, narrow opening in a surface. We sometimes put letters into a mail slot or money into a coin slot.
   a. What is the meaning of *insert*? _____
   b. Do you think Margie does her homework on paper or on something else? Why? _____

   _____

3. Margie put her homework into the computer "with a sigh." These words show how she was feeling. Consider what Margie is thinking about. What do you think *a sigh* means? Check (✓) your answer.
   ☐ a big smile   ☐ an angry shout   ☐ a sad or tired sound

4. How do you think Margie feels about the way education has changed since the school days of her grandfather's grandfather? _____

   _____

Summarizing

On a piece of paper, write a one-paragraph summary of "Technology in Science Fiction." Include answers to the following questions. If you wish, you can begin:

The reading "Technology in Science Fiction" defines "science fiction" as . . .

- What does *science fiction* mean?
- Who was one of the first writers of science fiction?
- Who was Jules Verne?
- What were some of the things that Jules Verne accurately predicted in his stories?
- What happened with science fiction during the twentieth century?

EXPANDING VOCABULARY

New Contexts

A Complete the sentences with the target words and phrases in the box. There are two extra words or phrases.

adventure	criminals	in spite of	society
century	descriptions	made up	style
confused	imaginations	predicted	took off

1. Jules Verne died in 1905, more than a _____ ago.

2. The actor didn't like his real name, so he _____ another.

3. Some people enjoy taking risks. They want exciting experiences. They go looking for _____.

4. We _____ that they would solve the problem, and they soon did.

5. She told her students to use their _____ to find a solution.

6. It is the job of the police to catch _____.

7. _____ expects people to obey the law and respect the rights of others.

8. The twins look so much alike that I can't be sure who's who. I get _____.

9. He volunteered to do the job _____ the danger.

10. The plane _____ from Madrid several hours ago. In a little while, it will land in Mexico City.

B   **Read these sentences. Write the boldfaced target words or phrases next to their definitions. There is one extra definition. Put an X next to it.**

a. I like the **style** of that car but not the color.

b. H_2O is a **scientific** term for water.

c. He gave the police a full **description** of the robber.

d. Sales have **neither** increased **nor** decreased. They have stayed exactly the same.

e. He dreamed of traveling in **outer space**, of going to the moon and beyond.

Target Words or Phrases	Definitions
1. _____	= not (one person, thing, or action) and not (another) either
2. _____	= the way something is made or done
3. _____	= relating to science or using its methods
4. _____	= a trip in a plane or spaceship
5. _____	= the area outside Earth's air, also called simply *space*
6. _____	= a piece of writing or speech giving details of what someone or something is like

Building on the Vocabulary: Word Grammar

After the phrase *in spite of*, you can use:

- a noun: *In spite of his injury, he stayed in the game and kept playing.*
- a pronoun: *The weather was bad, but we went out in spite of it.*
- a gerund (the *-ing* form of a verb used as a noun): *I went to class in spite of feeling sick.*

Write three statements using *in spite of*.

1. _____

2. _____

3. _____

Using New Words

Work with a partner. Choose five target words or phrases from the chart on pages 144–145. On a piece of paper, use each word or phrase in a sentence.

PUTTING IT ALL TOGETHER

Sharing Opinions

Answer the following questions. Then form a small group and find out the answers of the others in your group. Share the information about your group with the class.

1. Do you like to read science fiction:

In your first language? ☐ Yes ☐ No

In English? ☐ Yes ☐ No

2. Do you enjoy science fiction movies? ☐ Yes ☐ No ☐ Sometimes

Examples of sci-fi movies you have seen: _____

_____

3. What do you like or dislike about science fiction?

I like _____.

I don't like _____.

Writing

Choose a topic. Write a paragraph.

1. Margie, the little girl in Asimov's story "The Fun They Had," knows a little about her grandfather's grandfather's life when he was a boy. What do you know, and what can you imagine, about the lives of any of your great-great-grandparents?

2. Become a science fiction writer! Imagine your life thirty years from now. Think especially about the technology you will use every day. Describe something from your daily life.

UNIT 3 Wrap-up

REVIEWING VOCABULARY

Complete the phrase.

1. Write the noun phrase *a container for, methods of,* or *a solution to.*

   a. _____ a problem

   b. _____ a liquid

   c. _____ transportation

2. Write the verb *attend, predict,* or *repair.*

   a. _____ a car

   b. _____ a class

   c. _____ the future

3. Write the adjective *complex, rural,* or *valuable.*

   a. _____ jewelry

   b. a _____ situation

   c. a _____ area

4. Write the noun *applications, screens,* or *stories.*

   a. make up _____

   b. fill out _____

   c. measure _____

5. Write the adjective *accurate, equal,* or *modern.*

   a. an _____ report

   b. _____ amounts

   c. _____ society

6. Write the verb *rob*, *solve*, or *subtract*.

    a. _____ an amount

    b. _____ a problem

    c. _____ a bank

7. Write the noun *events*, *grain*, or *shadows*.

    a. dark _____

    b. recent _____

    c. fields of _____

EXPANDING VOCABULARY

Antonyms

Antonyms are words with opposite meanings, like *always* and *never*, *help* and *hurt*, or *break* and *repair*.

Sometimes a word takes a prefix that creates an antonym, like *agree* and *disagree* or *happy* and *unhappy*.

 Use one word from each pair of adjective antonyms to complete the sentences.

accurate—inaccurate	normal—abnormal
appropriate—inappropriate	regular—irregular
equal—unequal	similar—dissimilar

1. John is now working a _____ schedule, with every Sunday and Monday off.

2. You can't wear that shirt to your job interview! It's _____.

3. Older men often lose their hair, but hair loss in a child is _____.

4. The report was full of mistakes. It was highly _____.

5. He broke the candy bar into two _____ parts and gave me the smaller one.

6. The scientists expected _____ results, and they were right: The numbers were almost exactly the same.

 B   **Use one word from each pair of adjective antonyms to complete the sentences.**

complex—simple	rural—urban
high-tech—low-tech	valuable—worthless

1. The car was in such poor repair that it was almost _____.

2. There are many people, businesses, and big buildings in _____ areas.

3. Any marriage is a _____ relationship and difficult for others to understand.

4. My favorite tool for writing is fairly _____: It's a pencil.

A Puzzle

Complete the sentences with words you studied in Chapters 9–12. Write the words in the puzzle.

Across

2. Cars are bad for the
   e_____.

3. No one can swim in that lake anymore. There's too much
   p_____.

6. When my friend moved away, I felt a great sense of
   l_____.

7. We are living in the twenty-first
   c_____.

8. Yoko got her hair cut in a new
   s_____.

9. Bring your friends to eat with us—we have p_____ of food.

10. Tom is always traveling to exciting places. He loves a_____.

Down

1. I didn't understand what was happening. I felt c_____.

3. A laptop computer is more p_____ than a desktop model.

4. I want to be a better tennis player. How can I i_____ my skills?

5. Your boss doesn't pay you enough. You d_____ more.

7. Living near the airport, they have the c_____ sound of planes overhead.

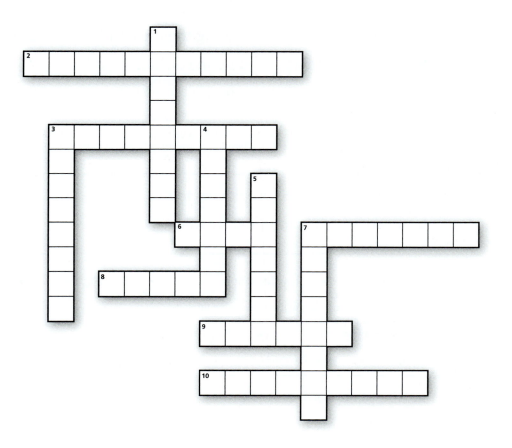

BUILDING DICTIONARY SKILLS

Look at the dictionary entries below. Then read each sentence and write the number of the meaning.

> **con•flict¹** /ˈkɑnˌflɪkt/ *n* **1** [C,U] angry disagreement between people, groups, countries, etc.: *a* **conflict between** *father and son* | **conflicts over** *land* | *The two groups have been* **in conflict with** *each other for years.* **2** [C,U] fighting or a war: **Armed conflict** *might be unavoidable.* | *efforts to* **resolve** *the* **conflict 3** [C,U] a situation in which you have to choose between opposing things: *a* **conflict between** *the demands of one's work and one's family* **4** [C] something that you have to do at the same time that someone wants you to do something else: *Sorry –* **I have a conflict** *Friday. Can we do it on Monday?* **5 conflict of interest(s)** a situation in which you cannot do your job fairly because you are personally affected by the decisions you make: *She sold her shares in the company to avoid any conflict of interest.*

1. _____ **a.** I can't make it to the meeting tomorrow. I have a conflict.

_____ **b.** The two partners ended up in constant conflict.

_____ **c.** At first, the conflict was limited to just those two nations.

> **fair•ly** /ˈfɛrli/ *adv* **1** more than a little, but much less than very: *She speaks English fairly well.* | *The recipe is fairly simple.* **2** in a way that is fair and reasonable: *I felt that I hadn't been treated fairly.*

2. _____ **a.** Do they treat their employees fairly?

_____ **b.** It was a fairly traditional wedding.

> **take off**
> **1 take** sth ↔ **off** to remove something [≠**put on**]: *Your name has been taken off the list.* | *Take your shoes off in the house.*
> **2** if an aircraft takes off, it rises into the air from the ground
> **3** *informal* to leave a place: *We packed everything in the car and took off.*
> **4 take time/a day/a week etc. off** also **take time, etc. off work** to not go to work for a period of time: *I'm taking some time off work to go to the wedding.*
> **5** to suddenly become successful: *He died just as his film career was taking off.*

3. _____ **a.** The plane took off on time.

_____ **b.** I took off my coat.

_____ **c.** He was here a moment ago, but then he took off.

_____ **d.** She took a month off after having her baby.

> **var•y** /'vɛri, 'væri/ *v* (**varied, varies**) **1** [I] if several things of the same type vary, they are all different from each other: *Prices* **vary from** *$10 to $50.* | *The flowers* **vary in** *color and size.* | *Test scores varied widely from child to child.* **2** [I] to change often: *The price of seafood* **varies according to** *the season.* | *"How often do you play tennis?" "Oh,* **it varies***."* **3** [T] to regularly change what you do or the way you do it: *You need to vary your diet.* —**varying** *adj*: *varying degrees of success*

4. ____ **a.** The teacher varied the class, so we didn't get bored.

   ____ **b.** The weather varies a lot in the spring.

   ____ **c.** The movies he makes don't vary much, do they?

> **load**¹ /loʊd/ *n* [C] **1** a large quantity of something that is carried by person, a vehicle, etc.: *a ship carrying* **a** *full* **load of** *fuel and supplies* **2 carload/truck load etc.** the largest amount or number that a car, etc. can carry: *a busload of kids* **3** the amount of work that a machine or a person has to do: *a light/heavy* **work load** **4** a quantity of clothes that are washed at the same time: *Can you* **do a load of** *clothes later today?*
> **SPOKEN PHRASES 5 a load of sth/loads of sth** a lot of something: *Don't worry, there's loads of time.* **6 get a load of sb/sth** said when you want someone to notice something funny or surprising

5. ____ **a.** Her business partner is sick, so her work load has increased.

   ____ **b.** There's already a load in the washing machine.

   ____ **c.** That's a heavy load of books in your backpack!

THE
ENVIRONMENT

13

Small Ride, Big Trouble

A tuk-tuk in the streets of Bangkok

GETTING READY TO READ

Talk about these questions with a partner or with your class.

1. Match these words with their definitions: *a pollutant, pollute, pollution.*

   a. _____ = make air, water, soil, etc., dangerously dirty and not good enough for people to use

   b. _____ = the process of making something dangerously dirty, or the substances that make it unsafe to use

   c. _____ = a substance that is produced by factories, cars, etc., and makes air, water, or soil, etc., dangerously dirty

2. How many different kinds of pollution can you name? Are any of them a problem where you live?

3. The reading in this chapter will be about pollution. Judging by the photo above, what kind of pollution do you think it will focus on?

READING

Look at the pictures, words, and definitions next to the reading. Then read without stopping. Don't worry about new words. Don't stop to use a dictionary. Just keep reading!

Small Ride, Big Trouble

1   Mary Jane Ortega, the mayor of San Fernando City in the Philippines, knew that her city was choking.[1] The cause? Air pollution, especially pollution from two- and three-wheeled **vehicles** like scooters,[2] motorcycles, and *tuk-tuks*.[3]

[1] *choking* = unable to breathe because there is not enough air

[2] a *scooter* = a small motorcycle

[3] a *tuk-tuk* See the photo on page 160.

2   The World Health Organization **estimates** that air pollution kills 2 million people a year. While big vehicles often get the blame for it, much of the blame in Asia really belongs to the "little guys." Small vehicles with two-stroke **engines** put out huge amounts of dangerous gases and oily black smoke. Cars, with their bigger, four-stroke engines, are actually cleaner and do less **harm** to the environment. In fact, one two-stroke engine vehicle can produce as much pollution as fifty cars.

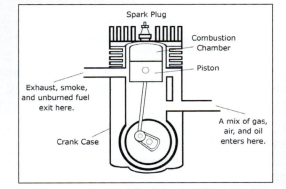

A diagram of a two-stroke engine*

3   Mayor Ortega thought that the solution was to get rid of the two-strokes. She offered **interest**-free **loans** to help people pay for new vehicles with four-stroke engines. Within three years, there were 400 of them on the streets of San Fernando. But there were still more than 800 of the two-strokes. Even with a loan, the change to a four-stroke was just too expensive for many people. (Two-stroke engines are lighter and simpler, so they are less expensive to buy and **maintain**.) Another problem was that the people who did change to a four-stroke were selling their old two-stroke to someone else in the city. The loans had brought about no **decrease** in either the number of two-strokes or the pollution. San Fernando needed another solution, and it had to be cheap.

---

* Go online and search "two-stroke engine animation" to see how a two-stroke engine works.

(continued)

4   **Meanwhile**, in Colorado (USA), a team of college students was trying to win a **competition**. They were developing a clean, two-stroke-engine snowmobile[4] for use in Yellowstone National Park. The team built a winning snowmobile that led to the start-up of a nonprofit business, Envirofit.

[4] a *snowmobile*

5   Using technology developed for the snowmobile, Envirofit came up with a way to retrofit two-stroke engines. *Retrofit* means to improve a machine by putting new and better parts in it (after it is already made). The company designed a retrofit kit—a set of parts and tools for people to use on their own two-stroke engines. Using the kit could cut down on the pollutants in the exhaust.[5] It could also help the engine make better use of **fuel**.

[5] *exhaust* = the gas produced by a working machine

6   The company sent kits to the Philippines to be tested by thirteen taxi drivers. Each driver had a three-wheeled motorbike with a sidecar for **passengers**. After eight months, the results were great. Using the kits had cut both pollution (by more than 70 percent) and the waste of gas and oil. Saving money on fuel turned the taxi drivers into believers. They found that using the kit could mean increasing their **income** by as much as a third. Right away, they started to spread the word[6] among other drivers.

[6] *spread the word* = tell others the news

7   Rolando Santiago, president of a taxi drivers' **association**, was one of the first drivers to retrofit his engine. He says, "After six months of using the kit, my extra income helped me save for a matching house grant.[7] I rebuilt my home and my neighbor's home, which provided better housing for six families." Santiago's story gives one example of how better air can lead to a lot of other better things.

[7] a *grant* = an amount of money given for a particular purpose

8   Few two-stroke-engine vehicles are in use in the United States. However, the United States has good reason to care about the harm these vehicles do. Pollution pays no attention to **borders** between countries or continents. For that reason, the U.S. government has spent thousands of dollars on kits for cities in India and other parts of Asia that have major air pollution problems. Pollution in India or the Philippines is not just their national problem, and pollution in Asia is not just Asia's problem.

ADAPTED FROM: "Two Strokes and You're Out" by David Kushner, *Discover Magazine*, May 2008.

Quick Comprehension Check

Read these sentences. Circle T (true) or F (false).

1. Two-stroke engines cause major air pollution.   T   F

2. Four-stroke engines cause twice as much pollution as two-strokes.   T   F

3. Two-stroke engines are cheaper than four-stroke engines.   T   F

4. You can fix a two-stroke so it causes less pollution.   T   F

5. The taxi drivers who tried the kits were happy with them.   T   F

6. Two-stroke engines are used only in the Philippines.   T   F

EXPLORING VOCABULARY

Thinking about the Target Vocabulary

A   **Find the twelve nouns and two verbs in bold in "Small Ride, Big Trouble." Add them to the chart. Write them in the order they appear in the reading. Use the singular form of any plural noun. Use the base form of each verb.**

	Nouns	Verbs	Adjectives	Other
1				
2				
3				

	Nouns	Verbs	Adjectives	Other
4				meanwhile
5				
6				
7				
8				

B **Which words are new to you? Circle them here. Then find them in the reading. Look at the context. Can you guess the meaning?**

Using the Target Vocabulary

A Complete these sentences **about the reading.** Use the words in the box.

association	decrease	fuel	income	meanwhile
borders	estimate	harm	loan	vehicles

1. Things that are used to carry people and goods from one place to another—like cars, scooters, buses, and trucks—are called

   _____.

2. The World Health Organization cannot know exactly how many people die from air pollution, but they _____ 2 million a year.

3. Two-stroke engines are worse for air quality than four-stroke engines. They do more _____.

4. People in San Fernando City got money to buy new four-stroke vehicles. Over time, they had to pay the money back. It was not a gift—it was a _____.

5. Unfortunately, the loans did not result in fewer two-stroke-engine vehicles. The loans did not lead to a _____ in two-strokes.

6. Two things were happening at the same time. People in San Fernando City were dealing with air pollution from two-strokes. _____, a team of U.S. college students was developing a clean two-stroke engine.

7. The taxi drivers' three-wheeled motorbikes burn gasoline to produce energy. Gasoline is one kind of _____. Others are wood, gas, and coal.

8. The Envirofit retrofit kit helped the Philippine taxi drivers earn more money. They were able to increase their _____.

9. Rolando Santiago is the leader of a taxi drivers' group. He is the president of their _____.

10. Air pollution doesn't care about the lines that divide one country from another. Air pollution does not respect _____.

B Read each definition and look at the paragraph number. Look back at the reading on pages 161–162 to find the **boldfaced** word to match the definition. Write it in the chart.

Definition	Paragraph	Target Word
1. the parts of vehicles or machines that produce power to make them move	2	
2. money that you pay for the use of someone else's money (like a bank's)	3	
3. keep something in good condition	3	
4. a situation in which people or groups try to beat each other to win something	4	
5. people who are traveling in a car, bus, plane, etc., but are not driving it	6	

DEVELOPING READING SKILLS

Cause and Effect

- Use *because* + a subject and a verb.

  Many people prefer motorcycles or scooters to cars

  <u>subject</u>   +   <u>verb</u>

  because <u>the smaller vehicles</u> <u>do not cost</u> as much.

- Use *because of* + a noun or noun phrase only (no verb).

  The taxi drivers saved money **because of** <u>the kit</u>.

 Complete each sentence about the reading.

1. The World Health Organization estimates that _____
   people die each year because _____.

2. San Fernando City had a bad problem with air pollution because

   _____.

3. Two-stroke engines are worse than four-stroke engines because _____

   _____.

 Find two more cause-effect relationships in the reading. On a piece of paper, write two sentences with *because* or *because of*.

Problem and Solution

Complete the chart with information from the reading.

Problem	Solutions Tried	Results
bad air quality—pollution from two-stroke engines	1.	
	2.	

Understanding Point of View

> It is important to understand a writer's **point of view**—the particular way that he or she thinks about or judges a subject. Sometimes a writer states his or her opinion directly; in other cases, the reader has to infer it.

Which statement best describes the writer's point of view?

☐ **1.** The writer thinks you have to pay people if you want them to stop polluting.

☐ **2.** The writer thinks people everywhere should know and care about air pollution in Asia.

☐ **3.** The writer thinks competitions are the way to find solutions to our problems with pollution.

EXPANDING VOCABULARY

New Contexts

 These sentences use the target words **in new contexts**. What is the meaning of each **boldfaced** word? Circle a, b, or c.

1. The painter **estimated** that the job would take three days. *Estimated* means

   a. promised.   **b.** doubted.   **c.** guessed.

2. We were working hard to clear away the snow. **Meanwhile**, another storm was coming our way. *Meanwhile* means

   a. earlier.   **b.** at the same   **c.** afterwards.
                             time.

3. This cough medicine may not help, but it won't do you any **harm**. If something does harm, it

   a. causes trouble   **b.** improves a   **c.** helps something last.
      or injury.   situation.

4. Your food is **fuel** for your body. A fuel is something that

    a. makes you gain weight.   **b.** keeps a person healthy.   **c.** produces heat or energy.

5. Your car will last longer if you **maintain** it. *Maintain it* means

    a. drive it slowly.   **b.** take care of it.   **c.** not use it.

6. A **decrease** in production costs can bring a company an increase in profits. If there is a decrease in something, there is

    a. less of it.   **b.** plenty of it.   **c.** more of it.

7. Can you help me with these **income** tax forms? *Income* means

    a. sales.   **b.** production.   **c.** earnings.

 B These sentences also use the target words **in new contexts**. Complete them with the words in the box. There are two extra words.

| association | competition | fuels | interest | passengers |
| border | engine | harm | loan | vehicles |

1. Solar-powered _____ run on energy from the sun.

2. Please turn off the car while you wait. Don't leave the _____ running.

3. You must show your passport if you want to cross the _____.

4. Who won first place in the piano _____?

5. Pay your credit card bill in full each month to avoid paying _____.

6. First-class _____ on an airplane have more comfortable seats.

7. A college or university's alumni _____ is a group for its graduates.

8. A mortgage is a _____ you get from a bank so you can buy a house or apartment.

Building on the Vocabulary: Word Grammar

> These words all relate to money:
>
> *loan*   *n.* an amount of money you get to use for a period of time: *a student loan, a new car loan*
>
>   *v.* (informal) give someone a loan: *Can you loan me some money?*
>
> *borrow*   *v.* to take money or something else to use and give back later: *Dan borrowed a book from me.* –*borrower n.*
>
> *lend*   *v.* to let someone borrow money or something else: *Could you lend me a pen?* (simple past: *lent*) –*lender n.*

 A Complete the sentences with *borrowed*, *borrowers*, *lenders*, *lent*, and *loans*.

1. Jack _____ some money to his brother but never got it back.

2. Paula _____ money from the bank to start her business.

3. How much interest do you have to pay on your _____?

4. Banks are the major _____ in the housing market.

5. _____ have to pay interest on bank loans.

B On a piece of paper, write three sentences. Use any of the forms of *borrow*, *lend*, and *loan*.

Using New Words

Work with a partner. Choose five target words from the chart on pages 163–164. On a piece of paper, use each word in a sentence.

PUTTING IT ALL TOGETHER

Discussion

Talk about these questions in a small group or with your class.

1. What is your opinion of the drivers of two-stroke-engine vehicles described in the reading? Choose one:

   a. They don't realize that they are polluting the air.

   b. They know but they don't care that they are polluting the air.

   c. _____

2. What kinds of transportation are available to you? What kinds of transportation do you normally use? What are their effects on the environment? How much does that influence the choices you make?

3. If people are doing something that causes pollution, how do you get them to change? Give examples to support your ideas.

Writing

Choose a topic. Write a paragraph.

1. Tell what kind of pollution worries you most and explain why. What should be done about the problem?

2. Does a sense of responsibility for the environment affect the choices you make in your everyday life? Explain what you do and why.

3. Write about question 2 or 3 from **Discussion** above.

CHAPTER 14

Your Trees, My Trees, Our Trees

Enjoying the shade

GETTING READY TO READ

Talk with a partner or in a small group.

1. What products can you think of that are made from trees? Make a list.

2. In what other ways are trees useful to people?

3. Which statement do you think is true?

   a. There are more trees than human beings on Earth.

   b. There are about as many trees as human beings.

   c. There are fewer trees than human beings.

READING

Look at the picture, words, and definitions next to the reading. Then read without stopping.

Your Trees, My Trees, Our Trees

1   Trees can be very beautiful, but they do much more than stand there looking nice and giving us **shade** for picnics.[1] In fact, trees are so valuable that it is hard to see how we could exist without them.

2   First, trees supply us with **oxygen**. When we breathe in air, our bodies use the oxygen from it, and then we breathe out **carbon dioxide**. Trees make wonderful partners for us because they do the opposite: They put oxygen into the air. They also take carbon out of the air and use it to produce wood and leaves. Keeping that carbon out of the air is a good thing because carbon dioxide is a greenhouse gas.[2]

3   Second, trees help clean up the environment. For example, they take pollutants out of the air, both dangerous gases (like carbon monoxide[3]) and dust we do not want to breathe in. According to the International Society of Arboriculture (ISA), in one year, the average tree takes four to five kilograms of pollution from the air. Trees clean the **soil** as well. Sometimes they pull pollutants out of the soil and store them, and sometimes they actually change pollutants so they do less harm. Trees can help with **urban** noise pollution, too. They are surprisingly good at blocking noise that comes from traffic, airports, and so on.

4   Third, trees can help in places at risk of flash **floods**—sudden floods caused by heavy rain. Trees help because their leaves break the force of rain and wind on the soil and their roots can take in huge amounts of water. When trees slow down rainwater from rushing across the ground, the water carries away less soil and in general does less harm. Also, by slowing the water down, trees give it time to pass from the surface down into underground aquifers.[4]

5   The list of **benefits** from trees goes on and on, but let's return to our first one: the effect of trees on our oxygen supply. The ISA estimates that one acre[5] of forest puts out four tons of oxygen a year. That, they say, is enough to meet the needs of 18 people. So, if one acre of forest is enough for 18 of us, how many acres does it take to meet the needs of the whole world? If you want to, you can find out how many people there are on Earth right now and do the math. However, every year, there are more and more of us. Is the tree **population** keeping up, or are we consuming trees faster than we are replacing them?

[1] a *picnic* = a meal eaten outdoors, as in a park

[2] *greenhouse gases* = gases that keep heat from escaping into space

[3] *carbon monoxide* = a poisonous gas produced by engines burning gasoline

[4] an *aquifer* = an underground layer of stone or earth that holds water

[5] an *acre* = a measure of land (about 4,047 square meters)

6   Ecology[6] professor Nalini Nadkarni wondered about this, so she **looked into** how many trees there are in the world. She knew that scientists had estimated the number of trees by looking at photos of Earth taken by satellites.[7] As of 2005, they estimated that we had about 400,246,300,000 trees. Nadkarni then wondered how many trees that meant per person. To get an answer, she divided the number of trees by the world's human population, and she found that there were 61 trees per person.

7   Was that good news or bad? Nadkarni started thinking about how many trees she herself would use in her lifetime. One of her students reported that each year, the average American uses the amount of wood in a 100-foot-tall tree that is 18 inches in **diameter**. Nadkarni thought about things she uses that are made from wood, or from other tree-based products, such as **rubber**. There are newspapers, magazines, movie tickets, birthday cards, pencils, **ink**, rubber boots, furniture, wooden chopsticks[8] . . .

8   Chopsticks? Nadkarni herself probably does not use a great number of those. However, she learned that every year, the Japanese throw away over 20 billion pairs of them. These chopsticks, called *wari-bashi* ("little quick ones"), are made of wood that comes from Vietnam, Malaysia, Thailand, the United States, and Canada. The Chinese throw away even more of them: 450 billion pair a year. That equals about 25 million trees. Every year.

9   Nadkarni does not tell this story to make chopstick users feel bad, or anyone else who is a major tree-consumer. She says, "I don't want people to feel guilty[9] about their relationships with trees and say, 'Oh, I can never touch another tree-created product again!'" She does want people to feel **grateful** that trees are such a wonderful **resource**. Let's remember, too, that trees are a **renewable** resource. If you may be using up more than your 61 trees—or if you worry that your oxygen supply is at risk—do something about it. Go out and plant some trees!

Professor Nadkarni's words come from "Going Out on a Limb with a Tree-Person Ratio" by Robert Krulwich. National Public Radio. Retrieved January 1, 2009, from http://www.npr.org/templates/story/story.php?storyId=96758439&sc=emaf.

[6] *ecology* = the study of plants, animals, people, and the environment

[7] a *satellite* = a machine circling Earth in space to send/receive information

[8] *chopsticks*

[9] *guilty* = feeling bad because you've done something you know is wrong

Quick Comprehension Check

Read these sentences. Circle T (true) or F (false).

1. Trees are good for air quality.	T	F
2. Trees and humans are in competition for air.	T	F
3. Trees help clean up the environment.	T	F
4. There are more people on Earth than trees.	T	F
5. Professor Nadkarni is upset with the makers of chopsticks.	T	F
6. She wants everyone to stop using tree-based products.	T	F

EXPLORING VOCABULARY

Thinking about the Target Vocabulary

A   Find the eleven nouns, one verb, and three adjectives in **bold** in "Your Trees, My Trees, Our Trees." Add them to the chart. Use the singular form of any plural noun. Use the base form of the verb.

	Nouns	Verbs	Adjectives	Other
1				
2				
3				
4				
5				

	Nouns	Verbs	Adjectives	Other
6				
7				
9				

B Which words and phrases are new to you? Circle them here. Then find them in the reading. Look at the context. Can you guess the meaning?

Using the Target Vocabulary

A Complete these sentences **about the reading**. Use the words in the box.

carbon dioxide	ink	resource	shade
diameter	oxygen	rubber	soil

1. A cooler area of shadow, created by a tree, for example, is called

   _____.

2. The gas in the air that is needed by all human beings, animals, and
   plants is _____.

3. _____ is the gas that people and animals
   breathe out.

4. The substance that trees and other plants grow in is
   _____. It is also sometimes called *earth* or *dirt*.

5. You can measure a tree by how wide it is—its _____ (a
   line drawn from one side of a circle to the other, through the center).

6. Certain trees contain a liquid that is used to make such things as
   car tires, rain boots, and basketballs. This material is called

   _____.

7. The liquid in a pen, or a colored substance in a computer printer, is called _____.

8. Trees are a valuable _____ (something that exists in a country and can be used in the production of other things).

 B These sentences are **about the reading.** What is the meaning of each **boldfaced** word or phrase? Circle a, b, or c.

1. Trees can help solve the problem of **urban** noise pollution. *Urban* means

   a. appropriate.   **b.** portable.   **c.** relating to cities.

2. Heavy rains can cause **floods**. When there is a flood, there is water
   a. in rivers and   **b.** in areas that   **c.** throughout a city.
       lakes.   are usually dry.

3. We get many **benefits** from trees. *Benefit* means
   a. a kind of fruit.   **b.** a natural   **c.** something that helps.
                                     product.

4. Which is greater, the world's human or tree **population**? *Population* means the number of
   a. products made   **b.** benefits from   **c.** living things in an
       from something.   something.   area.

5. Professor Nadkarni wanted information about the world's tree population, so she **looked into** it. *Looked into* means
   a. researched.   **b.** decreased.   **c.** estimated.

6. We should be **grateful** that we have trees. *Grateful* means
   a. careful.   **b.** thankful.   **c.** awful.

7. Trees are a **renewable** resource. If a resource is renewable, then we
   a. can replace it so   **b.** should avoid   **c.** are better off
       it isn't used up.   using it.   without it.

DEVELOPING READING SKILLS

Understanding Topics of Paragraphs

 A **Where in the reading is the information about each of these topics? Scan the reading and write the paragraph number.**

____5____ **a.** The oxygen production of trees

_____ **b.** Trees and pollution

_____ **c.** Trees and air quality

_____ **d.** Trees vs. floods

_____ **e.** Things made from tree-based products

_____ **f.** Trees used for chopsticks

_____ **g.** Advice for the reader

_____ **h.** The number of trees per person

B **On a piece of paper, write a sentence or two about each topic in Part A, beginning with the topic of paragraph 2 and continuing in order. Do not copy sentences from the reading. Use your own words.**

Example:

Paragraph 2: _Trees take carbon out of the air and put oxygen back into it._

Fact vs. Opinion

A **Decide if each statement is a fact or an opinion and circle Fact or Opinion. Base your answers on information from the reading.**

1. Trees have many benefits for human beings.	Fact	Opinion
2. Trees help limit greenhouse gases.	Fact	Opinion
3. Having 61 trees per person is not enough.	Fact	Opinion
4. People in developed countries use many tree-based products.	Fact	Opinion
5. We should not feel guilty about using trees.	Fact	Opinion
6. We can replace the trees we use.	Fact	Opinion

B   **Write two sentences.**

1. Write another fact about trees. If you use information from the reading, write a paraphrase or use quotation marks as needed.

   _____

   _____

2. Write an opinion of your own about trees.

   _____

   _____

EXPANDING VOCABULARY

New Contexts

 A   **Complete the sentences with the target words and phrases in the box. There are two extra words.**

benefits	floods	look into	population	resources
diameter	grateful	oxygen	renewable	urban

1. Rich countries generally have a lot of natural _____.

2. I don't know much about getting a bank loan, so I'll have to _____ it.

3. Your support has made a big difference, and I'm very _____.

4. Competition among stores brings _____ for consumers, such as lower prices.

5. A soccer ball is about 10 inches in _____.

6. _____ can do a lot of harm, but they can also be good for the soil.

7. Oil is not a _____ resource—we cannot make more of it.

8. George doesn't enjoy quiet rural areas; he likes the noise and activity of an _____ environment.

These sentences also use the target words in new contexts. Complete them with the words in the box. There are three extra words.

carbon dioxide	ink	population	rubber	soil
flood	oxygen	resource	shade	urban

1. When a patient has trouble breathing, a doctor may give him or her _____.

2. Air is made up of 78 percent nitrogen, 21 percent oxygen, and other gases including _____.

3. Before they had pens, people had to use a brush and _____ to write Chinese characters.

4. On a sunny day, it is cooler in the _____.

5. Rich _____ is good for growing plants.

6. In some countries, the birthrate is low but the _____ is growing because people are living longer lives.

7. _____ is a useful material for things that need to be waterproof.

Building on the Vocabulary: Studying Collocations

The noun *resources* is used in many different contexts. They include:	
natural resources	valuable things that naturally exist in a country (such as land, water, and minerals taken from the ground)
human resources	1. the abilities and skills of workers; 2. the office of a company that deals with employment, training, and helping employees
financial resources	the amount of money that a person or company has
educational resources	something that provides information to support teaching and learning

Complete each sentence with one of the phrases in the box on page 179.

1. The public library offers valuable _____.

2. Go to the _____ office to fill out an application.

3. Trees, unlike some other _____, are a renewable resource.

4. People without the _____ to pay for college can get loans.

Using New Words

Work with a partner. Choose five target words or phrases from the chart on pages 174–175. On a piece of paper, use each word or phrase in a sentence.

PUTTING IT ALL TOGETHER

Sharing Opinions

Talk about these questions with a partner or in a small group.

1. A statistic is a number that gives a fact or a measurement. The reading gives several statistics relating to trees. How many can you find? Which statistic is the most interesting to you and why?

2. Professor Nadkarni doesn't want people to feel guilty about their relationships with trees. Do you agree? How should we feel about trees?

Writing

Choose a topic. Write a paragraph.

1. Choose a statistic from "Your Trees, My Trees, Our Trees." Report the statistic and tell what you think about it. Include the source of the information.

   Examples:

   According to the International Society of Arboriculture, "one acre of forest puts out . . ."

   Ecology professor Nalini Nadkarni figured out that we have 61 trees per person in the world. That surprised me . . .

2. What, or who, are you grateful for? Why?

CHAPTER 15

Would You Eat Bugs to Save the World?

Do these look good to eat?

GETTING READY TO READ

Read the statements below and circle True or False. Then compare your answers with those of the class.

1.	Insects can be a good source of food.	True	False
2.	People in my country eat insects.	True	False
3.	I have seen people eat insects.	True	False
4.	I have eaten insects.	True	False
5.	I would be willing to try eating insects.	True	False

READING

Look at the pictures, words, and definitions next to the reading. Then read without stopping.

Would You Eat Bugs to Save the World?

1   Do you find it hard to imagine eating an insect? Perhaps you are saying to yourself, "Never in a million years would I eat bugs!" Or perhaps you are one of the many people who like to snack on grasshoppers.[1]

2   Human beings have eaten insects for thousands of years, and not just when they were **forced** to. The Romans ate them, and many modern cultures also consider them food. According to the United Nations (UN), people today eat over 1,400 species[2] of insects. They eat them in 29 countries in Asia, 36 countries in Africa, and 23 in the Americas. No doubt some of these people eat insects because they will go hungry **unless** they do, but many of them eat insects because they like the taste. Now there is another good reason to eat insects: to help the environment.

3   David Gracer eats insects, and he thinks you should, too. He **has set out** to **educate** people in the United States about eating them, especially in place of beef, chicken, and pork. The major reason to eat less of those foods is that **current** methods of **raising** livestock—animals such as cows, chickens, and pigs—have a terrible effect on the environment. A 2006 UN report made clear just how bad the situation is: Raising livestock is causing much of our water pollution, destroying large areas of land, and adding to global warming.[3] This is true for both huge U.S. factory farms and places where farmers can afford only a few animals. According to the report, raising cattle[4] produces more greenhouse gases[5] than cars and all other forms of transportation.

4   Raising insects, on the other hand, would cause far fewer **environmental** problems. At present, most edible[6] insects are not raised but rather harvested—that is, people go out into the forest to find them. All anyone needs to do is collect them and cook them. However, increased demand has led some farmers to start raising them, as in Thailand, where many types of insects are popular snacks.

[1] a *grasshopper*

[2] a *species* = a particular kind of plant or animal

[3] *global warming* = an increase in world temperatures

[4] *cattle*

[5] *greenhouse gases* = gases that keep heat from escaping into space, like carbon dioxide

[6] *edible* = safe to eat

5   David Gracer also points out some of the benefits that insects offer as food. For example, if you are trying to lose weight, you might like to know that grasshoppers contain only one-third the fat found in beef. Insects are also a good **source** of **protein**. Dried insects often have twice the protein of fresh fish.

6   **In terms of** protein, insects again compare well with beef. For every pound of grain that insects eat, they create far more protein than cattle do. Cattle have to eat several pounds of grain to produce just one pound of beef. In other words, cattle are not adding to the world's food supply—they are subtracting from it. Cattle also **require** huge amounts of another valuable resource, water. It takes 869 gallons of water to produce one-third of a pound of beef. (That will get you only one large hamburger.)

7   The idea of insects as food has the support of **experts**, such as Robert Kok, who teaches bioresource engineering[7] at McGill University in Montreal. Professor Kok has long spoken **in favor of** farming insects, and he sees them as a great source of protein, although he is not sure that many Canadians **are open to** the idea. Nutrition[8] professor Marion Nestle of New York University would agree. She thinks that before most North Americans would eat insects, they would have to be very, very hungry.

8   For now, David Gracer will continue to **speak out**—at schools and on TV and radio—on the benefits of eating insects. He realizes that change will come slowly, if at all, but he hopes one day to import[9] and sell edible insects, like the Mexican grasshoppers called *chapulines*. He will not try to make a living at it, however. He says, "If I did this for a living, my family and I would be eating bugs all the time."

[7] *bioresource engineering* = applying technology to problems in food production

[8] *nutrition* = getting the right foods for good health and growth

[9] *import* = bring something into a country (to sell it)

David Gracer's words come from "Want to Help the Environment? Eat Insects." by Josie Glausiusz, *Discover Magazine*, published online May 7, 2008.

Quick Comprehension Check

Read these sentences. Circle T (true) or F (false).

1. Members of many cultures around the world eat insects.   T   F

2. David Gracer is trying to teach people about insects as food.   T   F

3. Raising farm animals for meat is bad for the environment.   T   F

4. Insects have little real value as food.   T   F

5. Most North Americans seem willing to eat insects.   T   F

6. Gracer earns a good living selling insects for food.   T   F

EXPLORING VOCABULARY

Thinking about the Target Vocabulary

 A Find the three nouns, seven verbs, and two adjectives in **bold** in "Would You Eat Bugs to Save the World?" Add them to the chart. Use the singular form of any plural noun. Use the base form of each verb.

	Nouns	Verbs	Adjectives	Other
2				
				unless
3				
		*		
4				
5				
6				in terms of
7				
				in favor of
8				

Raising in paragraph 3 is a gerund. A gerund is the *-ing* form of a verb used as a noun, as in **Solving** problems is part of his job.

B Which words and phrases are new to you? Circle them in the chart on page 184. Then find them in the reading. Look at the context. Can you guess the meaning?

Using the Target Vocabulary

A Complete these sentences **about the reading**. Use the words and phrases in the box.

are open to	forced	in terms of	raise	speaking out
current	in favor of	protein	source	unless

1. Some people have eaten insects because they chose to, others because conditions _____ them to. They had no choice; there was nothing else to eat.

2. Some people will go hungry if they do not eat insects. They may even die of hunger _____ they eat them.

3. Farming methods in use at the present time are _____ methods.

4. When people, such as farmers, take care of animals or grow plants, especially to sell them, you can say that they _____ the animals or plants.

5. Insects can be a good food _____ (the place or thing that you get something from).

6. Insects, just like beef and fish, are a source of _____. This is a substance that is also found in eggs, beans, and milk and that helps your body grow.

7. Insects are better than beef when you consider them _____ protein—that is, when you think about them in that way.

8. Professor Robert Kok and other experts support the idea of farming insects. They are _____ this idea.

9. Professors Kok and Nestle doubt that North Americans

_____ the idea of eating insects. They don't think North

Americans are willing to think about it.

10. David Gracer means to go on _____ about why people

should raise insects for food rather than cattle, chicken, or pigs. He

will continue to speak publicly on something that he strongly

believes in.

B Read each definition and look at the paragraph number. Look back at the reading on pages 182–183 to find the **boldfaced** word or phrase to match the definition. Write it in the chart.

Definition	Paragraph	Target Word or Phrase
1. start (doing something, with a particular purpose or a goal in mind)	3	
2. teach someone	3	
3. relating to or affecting the land, air, or water on Earth	4	
4. need, demand	6	
5. people who know a lot about a subject from long study or experience	7	

DEVELOPING READING SKILLS

Understanding Main Ideas, Major Points, and Supporting Details

A reading generally has one main idea, with several **major points** to support that idea. It also has **supporting details** to support each major point. You can picture the relationships among the ideas this way:

Main Idea of the Reading					
Major Point		Major Point		Major Point	
Supporting Detail	Supporting Detail	Supporting Detail	Supporting Detail	Supporting Detail	Supporting Detail

Answer these questions.

1. What is the main idea of "Would You Eat Bugs to Save the World?"

   ☐ **a.** Eating insects has a long and respectable history.

   ☐ **b.** David Gracer wants people to change their eating habits.

   ☐ **c.** It could be good for the environment if more people ate insects.

2. Which sentences state major points of the reading, and which ones give supporting details? Write *MP* (major point) or *SD* (supporting detail).

   _MP_ **a.** Eating insects is normal in many cultures.

   _____ **b.** It takes 869 gallons of water to produce one-third of a pound of beef.

   _____ **c.** Insects have many benefits as food.

   _____ **d.** People around the world eat over 1,400 species of insects.

   _____ **e.** Experts support the idea of our eating insects.

   _____ **f.** A 2006 UN report said raising cattle is to blame for a lot of greenhouse gases.

   _____ **g.** Raising insects does little harm to the environment.

   _____ **h.** Grasshoppers have much less fat than beef.

Comparing and Contrasting

Use information from the reading to complete the diagram below. On the left, write facts about cattle and beef. On the right, write facts about insects as food. In the center, put things they have in common.

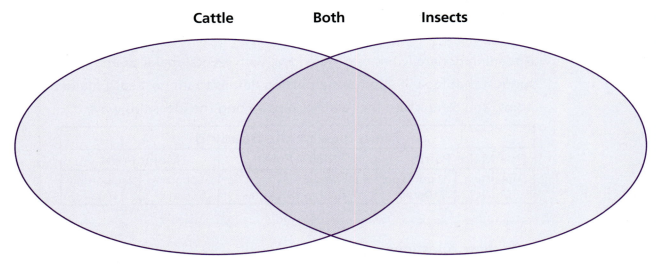

Cattle   Both   Insects

EXPANDING VOCABULARY

New Contexts

 A These sentences use the target words and phrases **in new contexts**. What is the meaning of each **boldfaced** word or phrase? Circle a, b, or c.

1. What—or who—would be a good **source** of information about renewable energy? A source is a person, place, or thing that
   a. supplies something.
   b. deserves something.
   c. causes harm.

2. Bad weather **forced** the airport to close. If you force people to do something, you
   a. let them do it.
   b. make them do it.
   c. ask them to do it.

3. The soil here is good for **raising** vegetables. *Raise* means
   a. grow.
   b. cook.
   c. maintain.

4. I haven't made up my mind. I'**m open to** suggestions. *To be open to something* means to be
   a. in need of it.   **b.** in charge of it.   **c.** willing to consider it.

5. Go online to find out about **current** weather conditions. *Current* means
   a. fast-moving.   **b.** uncertain.   **c.** present.

6. That car is too big, but **in terms of** passenger comfort, it's great. *In terms of* means
   a. in spite of.   **b.** on the subject of.   **c.** getting rid of.

7. Storing video on my computer **requires** a lot of memory. *Require something* means
   a. create it.   **b.** need it.   **c.** attend it.

B These sentences also use the target words and phrases **in new contexts**. Complete them with the words and phrases in the box. There are two extra words.

educated	experts	protein	set out	spoken out
environmentally	in favor of	raised	sources	unless

1. Things such as soaps and containers that do less harm to the environment are called "_____ friendly."
2. We cannot improve urban air quality _____ we can decrease pollution from all kinds of vehicles.
3. Your body uses _____ to make the red blood cells that carry oxygen.
4. Isn't everybody _____ getting rid of air pollution?
5. Henry feels that the situation is unfair, so he has _____.
6. We're depending on the _____ to come up with a solution.
7. In 1519, Ferdinand Magellan _____ to sail around the world.
8. Some science fiction writers have _____ their readers about technology and its effects on society.

Building on the Vocabulary: Word Grammar

> *Unless* often has the same meaning as *if . . . not*. For example, these two sentences have the same meaning:
>
> I won't eat a grasshopper **unless** you eat one, too.
>
> I won't eat a grasshopper **if** you do**n't** eat one, too.
>
> However, *unless* is usually used to refer to future conditions only. You must use *if . . . not*, not *unless*, in these examples:
>
> Past: **If** I had**n't** read the UN report, I wouldn't have believed him.
>
> Present: **If** insects did**n't** taste good, people in Thailand wouldn't eat them.

 A   **Complete the sentences.**

1. I'll be in class unless _____

2. You shouldn't do it unless _____

B   **On a piece of paper, write two sentences with *unless*.**

Using New Words

Work with a partner. Choose five target words or phrases from the chart on page 184. On a piece of paper, use each word or phrase in a sentence.

PUTTING IT ALL TOGETHER

Discussion

Talk in a small group.

1. Look back at the diagram on page 188. First, discuss the facts from the reading about cattle and insects: What is the same, and what is different? Then, share other information you have, and your own opinions, about raising cattle and eating beef versus raising and eating insects.

2. Look back at your answers on page 181. Do you want to change any of them? How have your ideas about eating insects changed (if at all)?

Writing

Choose a topic. Write a paragraph.

1. Write a short letter to David Gracer. Tell him what you think of his efforts to educate people about eating insects.

2. Have you ever spoken out about something you believed in with the result that people made fun of you or argued with you? Describe your experience.

CHAPTER 16

A Small Creature with a Big Job

A beekeeper and his honeybees

GETTING READY TO READ

Talk with a partner or in a small group.

1. What do you see happening in the photo above? How does this photo make you feel?

2. Do you know the words *pollen* and *hive*? See the pictures.

A honeybee collecting pollen

Wild bees outside their hive

A beekeeper's hives

3. What do you know about bees? Give some facts about bees and what they do.

READING

Look at the picture, words, and definitions next to the reading. Then read without stopping.

A Small Creature with a Big Job

1   Have you ever watched a bee at work on a flower? It wastes no time as it packs pollen onto its back legs to carry off to the hive. On their travels, bees carry pollen from flower to flower, pollinating[1] the plants, a process which allows the plants to produce fruit. The bee and the plant are partners in this process, each **essential** to the other—and to us.

[1] *pollinate* = make a flower or plant produce seeds by giving it pollen

2   One-third of the food we eat comes from plants that need animals to pollinate them. Birds do some of this work, but insects do most of it, and most of those insects are bees. Without the services of bees, we would have no tomatoes, soybeans, peppers, apples, melons, or pears, to name just a few bee-pollinated plants. If anything happened to the world's bee populations, that would be bad news for anyone who eats fruits or vegetables. Does that include you? Then you need to know that bees today are facing many **threats**.

3   Jeff Anderson knows a great deal about those threats. He has been a beekeeper for 30 years, ever since he married a beekeeper's daughter and went into the family business. Each year, he travels the United States with his bees, spending the spring among California fruit trees and summers in the fields of Minnesota. He is continuing a long tradition of beekeepers who move their hives with the seasons so their bees can **hunt** for new sources of pollen. In ancient[2] Egypt, beekeepers would transport their bees down the Nile River to find flowering **crops**. In North America, beekeepers over the years have traveled by covered wagon,[3] riverboat, and train. Transporting hives long distances became much easier with the development of major highways in the 1940s.

[2] *ancient* = existing very far back in history

[3] a *covered wagon*

4   Around that same time, another change **occurred**. Traveling beekeepers had been paying farmers to let them place hives on their land. However, wild bees were disappearing, until finally there were no longer enough wild bees left to pollinate the farmers' crops. That meant the farmers had to **call on** the beekeepers' bees to do the job instead. Then the farmers started paying the beekeepers.

(continued)

Today, billions of dollars' worth of U.S. crops depend on traveling beekeepers and their honeybees.

5   The wild bees were disappearing because of changes in land use and methods of farming. As more and more land was developed for housing, there were fewer and fewer flowering plants to feed wild bees. **Agriculture** was changing, too, with the introduction of new **pesticides**. Bees were carrying pollen with pesticides home to their hives and killing off entire populations.

6   North America is home to **at least** 4,500 different kinds of bees. The bees that Jeff Anderson and other beekeepers work with are European honeybees, which were brought over from Europe about 400 years ago. Their numbers have been dropping, too, and Anderson says it keeps getting harder to raise healthy bees. In the 1980s, honeybees came under attack from two types of parasites[4] that were new to North America. Pesticides have hurt honeybees, too. In the spring of 2005, U.S. beekeepers found that one-third of their bees had died during the winter.

[4] a *parasite* = an animal that lives on another and gets food from it

7   Saving wild bees may be the best hope for the long-term health of crops that depend on bees. However, wild bees face a problem that has to do with the way that farmland is managed. For example, one of the most **productive** farm regions in North America is California's Central Valley, **yet** this area is not at all welcoming to wild bees. Too little of the land is in its natural state. Farmers and homeowners there have put the land to their own uses and gotten rid of weeds,[5] which are rich sources of pollen for wild bees. Bee experts know that wild bees do best when farmers avoid chemical pesticides and leave some land in its natural state. These experts can tell farmers and other big landowners—and anyone with a garden—how to protect wild bees.

[5] *weeds* = wild plants growing where they are not wanted

8   The disappearing bee is only one of the many environmental **crises** in the news today. With all of these problems, just hearing the phrase *the environment* is enough to make us anxious.[6] Douglas Barasch, editor of the environmental magazine *OnEarth*, has thought a lot about this situation. He knows that news about the environment often sounds bad, yet he says he is not depressed.[7] Why not? Experience tells him that within each problem **lies** its solution. He is always meeting people who, when they see something "broken," **immediately** see an opportunity. They see a chance to fix something and make it better, whether it is a **motor** to be improved, a forest to be restored,[8] or a law to be changed. Yes, there are serious problems with our environment, but there are good solutions, too.

[6] *anxious* = very worried

[7] *depressed* = very sad

[8] *restored* = put back into good condition

Quick Comprehension Check

Read these sentences. Circle T (true) or F (false).

1. Bees carry pollen from one plant to another.   T   F

2. A beekeeper is a place where honeybees live.   T   F

3. Traveling beekeepers are not welcomed by farmers.   T   F

4. Modern farming methods have harmed bee
   populations.   T   F

5. Changes in land use are needed to protect bees.   T   F

6. No one who cares about the environment has any
   hope these days.   T   F

EXPLORING VOCABULARY

Thinking about the Target Vocabulary

A Find the six nouns, four verbs, and two adjectives in **bold** in "A Small Creature with a Big Job." Add them to the chart. Use the singular form of any plural noun. Use the base form of each verb.

	Nouns	Verbs	Adjectives	Other
1				
2				
3				
4				
5				
6				at least
7				
				yet

	Nouns	Verbs	Adjectives	Other
8	*			
				immediately

*The singular form of *crises* is *crisis*.

 B Which words and phrases are new to you? Circle them in the chart on pages 195–196. Then find them in the reading. Look at the context. Can you guess the meaning?

Using the Target Vocabulary

A These sentences are **about the reading**. What is the meaning of each **boldfaced** word? Circle a, b, or c.

1. Bees and bee-pollinated plants are **essential** to each other. *Essential* means

   a. quite similar.   **b.** very important.   **c.** artificial.

2. Traveling beekeepers move to places where their bees can **hunt** for new sources of pollen. *Hunt* means

   a. estimate.   **b.** look for.   **c.** require.

3. Some areas of farmland are very successful, **yet** wild bees cannot live there. *Yet* means

   a. because.   **b.** unless.   **c.** but.

4. The loss of bees is a **crisis** because many fruits and vegetables depend on bees for pollination. A crisis is

   a. a very bad situation that might get worse.   **b.** a chance to make some money.   **c.** a story about a new development.

5. Douglas Barasch believes that the solution to each environmental problem **lies** within it. In this sentence, *lies* means

   a. maintains.   **b.** deserves.   **c.** can be found.

6. When some people see an environmental problem, they **immediately** see a chance to do some good. *Immediately* means

a. right away.   **b.** naturally.   **c.** gratefully.

7. "A **motor** to be improved" is an example of something that needs to be fixed. A motor is

a. a kind of bee.   **b.** an engine.   **c.** an event.

B Complete these sentences **about the reading**. **Use the words and phrases in the box.**

agriculture	call on	occurred	productive
at least	crops	pesticides	threats

1. Bees today are facing many _____—things that are a danger to them and could do them serious harm.

2. Some farmers make a living by raising vegetables, grains, or fruit. The products that farmers grow for sale are their _____.

3. There were changes in transportation in the United States in the 1940s. Around that same time, a change _____ in the relationship between farmers and traveling beekeepers.

4. After wild bees started disappearing, and there weren't enough of them to pollinate crops, farmers had to _____ the European honeybee.

5. The science and work of farming is called _____.

6. Farmers often use chemicals to kill insects that would destroy their crops. These chemicals are called _____.

7. There are many kinds of bees in North America—_____ 4,500 kinds (meaning there may be more than—but not less than—that number).

8. California's Central Valley is famous in North America because so many crops grow there. It is a very _____ farm region.

DEVELOPING READING SKILLS

Text Organization

Number these events in chronological order, from 1 (the earliest) to 7 (the most recent).

_____ **a.** U.S. land was taken for housing and highways, and new pesticides came into use.

_____ **b.** Beekeepers in ancient Egypt transported their hives down the Nile River.

_____ **c.** Two new types of parasites attacked honeybees in North America.

_____ **d.** The European honeybee was imported into the United States.

_____ **e.** Wild bees began to disappear.

_____ **f.** U.S. beekeepers lost one-third of their bees during the winter.

_____ **g.** Farmers started paying traveling beekeepers for the services of their honeybees.

Understanding Main Ideas, Major Points, and Supporting Details

Answer these questions.

1. What is the main idea of "A Small Creature with a Big Job"?

   ☐ **a.** Bees have an essential role in the production of many crops.

   ☐ **b.** Bees are facing many threats, and we can't afford not to protect them.

   ☐ **c.** Environmental problems can be solved if we just listen to the experts.

2. Which of these sentences state major points of the reading, and which ones give supporting details? Write *MP* (major point) or *SD* (supporting detail).

    <u>MP</u> **a.** Bees play an important part in the lives of many plants.

    _____ **b.** There are at least 4,500 kinds of bees in North America.

    _____ **c.** U.S. agriculture depends on the services of beekeepers and their honeybees.

    _____ **d.** Beekeepers today are finding it difficult to raise healthy bees.

    _____ **e.** Apples, pears, and other fruit need bees to carry pollen from flower to flower.

    _____ **f.** Surprisingly, California's rich Central Valley is not a great place for wild bees.

    _____ **g.** Both wild bees and honeybees are in danger.

    _____ **h.** Farmers and gardeners don't like weeds, but bees do.

Understanding Point of View

Which statement best describes the point of view of the writer of "A Small Creature with a Big Job"?

☐ **1.** We are in a crisis and something terrible is going to happen.

☐ **2.** The situation is bad and will get worse unless we do something.

☐ **3.** There have been some problems, but there is no real need to worry.

EXPANDING VOCABULARY

New Contexts

A **Complete the sentences with the target words and phrases in the box. There are two extra words.**

agriculture	crises	hunt	lie	occur	threat
at least	crop	immediately	motor	pesticides	yet

1. Natural _____ do not contain chemicals.

2. When and where did the accident _____?

3. You could probably think of _____ twenty-five tree-based products you use.

4. The predicted ice storm presents a serious _____ to the farmer's apple trees.

5. An engine generally uses fuel, while a _____ can also be electric.

6. You don't have to repay the loan _____, but the interest starts adding up right away.

7. My grandfather forgets where he left his glasses, and then we all have to _____ for them.

8. The phrase *a bumper* _____ means a very large amount produced in one season.

9. The U.S. Secretary of _____ advises the president about farming, food production, and so on.

10. Experts say that insects can be good sources of protein, _____ many people are simply not open to the idea of eating them.

B Read these sentences. Write the **boldfaced** target words or phrases next to their definitions. There is one extra definition. Put an X next to it.

a. The experts predicted an economic **crisis**.

b. Flowers are **essential** to the bees' production of honey.

c. The manager knew who the most **productive** employees were.

d. The president **called on** everyone to avoid wasting electricity and fuel.

e. The engineer believed the answers **lay** in developing appropriate technologies.

Target Words or Phrases	Definitions
1. _____	= existed or could be found
2. _____	= needed, highly important
3. _____	= requiring a lot of resources
4. _____	= getting a lot of work done
5. _____	= a time when a situation is very bad or dangerous
6. _____	= formally asked someone to do something or to accept a responsibility

Building on the Vocabulary: Word Grammar

The verbs *occur*, *take place*, and *happen* have similar meanings.

- *Occur* means "happen" but is more formal. Use it to report past, unplanned events: *The accident occurred at 11:25 P.M. at Main Street and Broadway. Occur to* (someone) means "come into someone's mind, often suddenly."

- *Take place* means "happen" but is used for planned events, not things that happen by chance: *The wedding will take place in June.*

- *Happen* is used more often than the other verbs, usually for unplanned events: *What happened to your eye?*

Circle the best verb to use in each sentence. There may be more than one possible answer.

1. The meetings normally (occur / take place / happen) in the school library.

2. I don't understand what's (occurring / taking place / happening).

3. These events all (occurred / took place / happened) before I was born.

4. It didn't (occur / take place / happen) to me to check the pockets before washing my jeans.

 On a piece of paper, write three sentences. Use *occur*, *take place*, and *happen*.

Using New Words

Work with a partner. Choose five target words or phrases from the chart on pages 195–196. On a piece of paper, use each word or phrase in a sentence.

PUTTING IT ALL TOGETHER

Discussion

Talk with a partner or in a small group.

1. What has been happening to bees? What threats do they face?

2. Why should we care what happens to bees?

3. What other animals can you name that have disappeared or that are in danger of disappearing? Should something be done, or is this just the way the world works? Explain.

4. In paragraph 8, the writer states:

    The disappearing bee is only one of the many environmental crises in the news today. With all of these problems, just hearing the phrase *the environment* is enough to make us anxious.

    Do you think this is true? Do you think the writer is truly afraid for the future? Explain why or why not.

Writing

Choose a topic. Write a paragraph.

1. An optimist is a person who believes that good things will happen. A pessimist is the opposite: a person who expects that bad things will happen or that a situation will end badly. Which are you? Explain.

2. Do you prefer an urban or a rural environment? Or some other kind of environment? Explain what you prefer and why.

REVIEWING VOCABULARY

 A Think about the meanings of the words in each group below. Cross out the one word that does not belong in the group.

1. engine   vehicle   motor   protein

2. educator   passenger   border   expert

3. benefit   harm   threat   crisis

4. soil   ink   pesticide   agriculture

5. diameter   loan   income   interest

 B Complete each sentence with a word or phrase in the box. There are two extra words or phrases.

at least	carbon dioxide	in terms of	set out
be open to	hunt	look into	speak out
call on	in favor of		

1. The chemical symbol for _____ is CO$_2$.

2. Most people were too afraid of the government to _____.

3. I can't answer your question today, but I'll _____ it.

4. Georgia managed to do everything she _____ to do.

5. Has the boss already made a decision, or will he _____ other ideas?

6. I'm sure you could list _____ ten products made of rubber.

7. The United Nations must _____ all its members for support.

8. It is still a developing country, but it is rich _____ its natural resources.

EXPANDING VOCABULARY

Use words from word families 1 through 6 to complete the sentences below.

	Nouns	Verbs	Adjectives	Other
1	association	associate	associated	
2	competition competitor	compete	competitive	competitively
3	gratitude		grateful	gratefully
4	product production productivity	produce	productive	productively
5	renewal	renew	renewable	
6	requirement	require	required	

1. **a.** They are active members of their neighborhood _____.

   b. There are many health problems _____ with smoking.

2. **a.** The advertising business is highly _____.

   b. Who won the _____?

3. **a.** I _____ accepted her offer of a loan.

   b. We'd like to get him a gift, to express our _____ for his support.

4. **a.** New technology has helped farmers use their land more _____.

   b. Managers try to increase the _____ of their workforce.

5. **a.** *Urban* _____ means the process of improving poor areas of cities by building new housing, stores, etc.

   b. _____ energy includes solar power, for example.

6. **a.** Some U.S. college students have to meet a foreign language _____ before they can graduate.

   b. All living things _____ oxygen.

A PUZZLE

There are 12 target words from Unit 4 in this puzzle. The words go across (→) and down (↓). Find the words and circle them. Then use them to complete the sentences below. (Note: The words in the sentences are not in the same order as the words in the puzzle.)

X	E	Z	F	O	R	C	E	R	P	X
H	S	X	U	N	L	E	S	S	O	J
R	T	K	E	Z	J	X	W	G	P	Z
A	I	X	L	X	W	K	Z	S	U	Q
I	M	M	E	D	I	A	T	E	L	Y
S	A	E	S	S	E	N	T	I	A	L
E	T	X	C	Z	X	V	Q	X	T	I
D	E	C	R	E	A	S	E	K	I	E
K	X	V	Q	X	W	J	X	Z	O	S
Z	J	X	Z	C	U	R	R	E	N	T
M	E	A	N	W	H	I	L	E	Q	X

Across

1. There will be flooding _____ the rain stops soon.
2. Air and water are not just valuable—they are _____.
3. We must act _____ to deal with this threat.
4. The politicians kept on talking, and _____, the crisis grew.
5. No one can _____ him to do what he does not want to do.
6. The company cut workers' pay to bring about a _____ in its production costs.
7. I read the newspaper to educate myself on _____ events.

Down

1. Heating _____ costs have risen.
2. The world _____ is said to be well over 6 billion.
3. The solution _____ in getting everyone to work together.
4. The soil is too poor to _____ good crops there.
5. Multiply your income by 20 percent to _____ your tax.

BUILDING DICTIONARY SKILLS

Look at the dictionary entries below. Then read each sentence and write the number of the meaning.

> **main•tain** /meɪnˈteɪn/ *v* [T] **1** to make something continue in the same way or at the same standard as before: *The U.S. and Britain have maintained close ties.* | *It is important to maintain a healthy weight.* **2** to keep something in good condition by taking care of it: *It costs a lot of money to maintain a big house.* **3** to strongly express an opinion or attitude: *I've always maintained that any changes in the law will hurt the poor more than the rich.* | *From the beginning James has maintained his innocence.*

1. _____ **a.** The owner of the apartment building is responsible for maintaining it.

   _____ **b.** Experts maintain that insects can be good sources of protein.

   _____ **c.** They maintained a close friendship for the rest of their lives.

> **ben•e•fit¹** /ˈbɛnəfɪt/ *n* **1** [C] the money or other advantages that you get from something such as insurance or the government, or as part of your job: *The company provides medical benefits.* | *Social Security benefits* **2** [C,U] an advantage, improvement, or help that you get from something: *What are the benefits of contact lenses?* | *The new credit cards will be of great benefit to our customers.* | *Marc translated what the minister said for my benefit* (=to help me). **3** [C] a performance, concert, etc. that is done in order to make money for a CHARITY

2. _____ **a.** Tickets for the benefit have sold out.

   _____ **b.** *In your own best interest* means "of most benefit to you."

   _____ **c.** Speak to someone in Human Resources if you have questions about benefits.

> **shade¹** /ʃeɪd/ *n* **1** [singular, U] an area that is cooler, and darker because the light of the sun cannot reach it [→ SHADOW]: *Let's find a table in the shade* | *boys sitting in the shade of a tree* **2** [C] something that reduces or blocks light, especially a cover that you pull across a window **3** [C] a particular degree of a color: *a darker shade of red* **4 shades** [plural] *informal* SUNGLASSES **5 shade of meaning/opinion etc.** a meaning, etc. that is slightly different from other ones: *The word can have many shades of meaning depending on the context.*

3. _____ **a.** We pull down the shades at night.

   _____ **b.** It will be cooler in the shade.

   _____ **c.** I like that shade of blue.

   _____ **d.** People will argue over the shades of meaning in the president's statement.

Circle the letter of the word or phrase that best completes each sentence.

Example:

In most cars, the _____ is in the front of the vehicle.

a. transportation　　b. population　　c. engine　　d. technology

1. A news reporter must have many _____ of information.

   a. crops　　　　b. sources　　　c. loads　　　d. threats

2. A message appeared on my computer screen saying that a problem had _____.

   a. improved　　b. occurred　　c. solved　　d. harmed

3. _____ planning has to include housing, business, transportation, schools, and parks, among other things.

   a. Portable　　b. Valuable　　c. Renewable　　d. Urban

4. Your computer printer isn't broken—it just needs _____.

   a. conflict　　b. rubber　　c. ink　　d. fuel

5. Olga is in Dallas to _____ a meeting.

   a. attend　　b. subtract　　c. raise　　d. call on

6. There's a committee in charge of organizing all the _____.

   a. losses　　b. shades　　c. events　　d. proteins

7. We plan to go ahead with our trip _____ the bad weather they're predicting.

   a. in spite of　　b. in terms of　　c. unless　　d. meanwhile

8. Your personal _____ include not only your money but also your skills and time.

   a. containers　　b. grains　　c. adventures　　d. resources

9. After the rain, water continued to _____ from the trees.
   a. lie   **b.** pollute   **c.** drip   **d.** multiply

10. Naturally they're unhappy to see their daughter marry a _____.
    a. diameter   **b.** border   **c.** shadow   **d.** criminal

11. The long wait left everyone on the train feeling very _____.
    a. annoyed   **b.** modern   **c.** appropriate   **d.** essential

12. A travel writer must write detailed _____ of places.
    a. decreases   **b.** descriptions   **c.** experts   **d.** styles

13. When the bridge failed, some people _____ the engineers.
    a. blamed   **b.** robbed   **c.** educated   **d.** spoke out

14. They are now _____ that the flight will arrive thirty minutes late.
    a. repairing   **b.** estimating   **c.** improving   **d.** forcing

15. To write adventure stories, you need a good _____.
    a. motor   **b.** passenger   **c.** imagination   **d.** interest

16. Do you agree that we should judge a _____ by how it treats its
    weakest members—children, old people, and the sick?
    a. method   **b.** solution   **c.** crisis   **d.** society

17. A business must keep _____ records of all costs, profits, and losses.
    a. confused   **b.** accurate   **c.** grateful   **d.** equal

18. It's not just children who _____ others for being different.
    a. make fun of **b.** make up   **c.** fill out   **d.** vary

19. The stories told in many science fiction films take place in _____.
    a. carbon dioxide **b.** association   **c.** outer space   **d.** agriculture

20. Mark _____ to prove that he could make a difference, and he did.
    a. maintained   **b.** predicted   **c.** hunted   **d.** set out

21. My father was not an emotional man, _____ his tears flowed that
    day.
    a. yet   **b.** fairly   **c.** neither   **d.** at least

22. New inventions that need electricity are of no _____ to many people in developing countries.
   a. benefit   **b.** flood   **c.** oxygen   **d.** soil

23. The _____ method means doing careful testing and record keeping.
   a. constant   **b.** scientific   **c.** rural   **d.** productive

24. You can see all the latest _____ at the auto show.
   a. pesticides   **b.** loans   **c.** centuries   **d.** models

25. It _____ a great deal to employees to feel that they are treated fairly.
   a. deserves   **b.** takes off   **c.** matters   **d.** requires

26. Trees take in carbon dioxide and use it in the _____ of wood and leaves.
   a. income   **b.** plenty   **c.** production   **d.** competition

27. _____ groups have attacked the plan to allow houses to be built on the mountainside.
   a. Current   **b.** Environmental   **c.** Complex   **d.** High-tech

28. Maria was in love, but her friends disliked the man and told each other that she would _____ finding someone else.
   a. be better off   **b.** look into   **c.** be open to   **d.** be in favor of

See the Answer Key on page 265.

UNIT
5

ECONOMICS

CHAPTER 17

Economics— What's It All About?

Home buyers

GETTING READY TO READ

Talk about these questions with your class.

1. When you hear the words *the economy*—let's imagine from a TV news reporter—what topics do you expect the reporter to talk about?

2. Look at the photo above. How does it relate to the subject of economics?

3. How many people in the class have studied economics? What are some reasons to study this subject?

Look at the words and definitions next to the reading. Then read without stopping. Don't worry about new words. Don't stop to use a dictionary. Just keep reading!

Economics— What's It All About?

1   What do you think of when you hear the word *economics*? Perhaps the front page of a newspaper, where you might see stories about employment or interest rates or a national **debt** on the **rise**. Many people find that such stories use terms they do not understand. They find economics confusing, yet they feel they need to know something about it. We all do. After all, economics is about us. In the words of Canadian economist Jim Stanford, "Economics is about who does what, who gets what, and what they do with it."

2   When we talk about economics, we are talking about ourselves as workers, consumers, savers, borrowers, and investors. The results of our **individual** and collective[1] decisions in those roles make up **the economy**. Our individual decisions include such things as what products to buy, what work to do, and how much to invest in our education. To get the things we need and want, we need to use our resources—our money, time, and skills—and those resources are limited. That forces us to make choices.

[1] *collective =* shared or done by all the members of a group

3   Economist Pearl Claunch explains, "The economist's special way of looking at the world **involves** looking at the costs and benefits of making any decision or choice. Economics says that **since** everything interesting in life is **scarce**, choices have to be made. And choices involve costs as well as benefits. So if you want to make wise choices, you should use a benefit/cost **approach**."

4   This method of decision making, also called *cost-benefit analysis*, is often used by governments in deciding how to use their resources. Take the case of a decision about whether to build a highway. Officials[2] would estimate the costs of the project (in taxpayer money, for example) and compare them with the benefits (to highway users, for example). We can use the same approach in deciding how we spend our own money, or our time.

[2] an *official =* someone with a responsible job in an organization

5   However, the costs of buying or doing something include more than just the price we pay in dollars or euros or yen. When we choose one thing over another, we lose the **opportunity** to get

(continued)

that other thing we want. Economists have a term for this loss: *opportunity cost*. When you have a limited amount of money and you choose to spend it on a pizza instead of a movie, you have lost the chance to see the film. The opportunity cost of getting the pizza is not getting to see the movie.

6   To return to the example of the highway: When the government considers the cost to taxpayers, it must consider more than the price of **labor** and materials. Tax money is a scarce resource, and the government could use that money elsewhere.[3] In other words, what is the opportunity cost of building the highway? In addition, there are environmental costs to **take into account**, such as the loss of fields or forests. There may also be costs to people whose **property** lies in the way of the highway.

7   Spending decisions are only part of the government's role in the economy. One of its most basic responsibilities is creating currency (the economist's term for money), which lets us make trades for goods and services. Imagine if we had to **exchange** goods and services without the use of money, the way people did before money was invented. How would you pay your school for your classes? You could offer to trade the school some of your belongings[4] or do a job for them, but you might not have anything the school needed. Even if you did, you would waste a lot of time negotiating[5] the trade. Money, on the other hand, lets us buy and sell goods and services quickly and easily.

8   Most people agree that the government plays an essential role in creating and regulating[6] money. However, other parts of its role in the economy lead to much disagreement. Our individual values make us judge government actions differently, just as our values lead us to different choices in our own lives. We weigh the costs and benefits of government actions; we debate[7] what is and is not **necessary**. We all have opinions about who should do what, who should get what, and what they should do with it, and that is what economics is all about.

[3] *elsewhere* = in some other place

[4] *belongings* = things that someone owns

[5] *negotiate* = discuss in order to reach an agreement

[6] *regulate* = control an activity or process, usually by having rules

[7] *debate* = discuss something so as to make a decision about it

Quick Comprehension Check

Read these sentences. Circle T (true) or F (false).

1. Economics is about people—earners, spenders, investors, etc.   T   F

2. Your personal resources include your time and skills.   T   F

3. Limited resources force us to make choices.   T   F

4. Economists value a particular decision-making method.   T   F

5. Spending money is the government's most basic job.   T   F

6. Money makes our economic lives more difficult.   T   F

EXPLORING VOCABULARY

Thinking about the Target Vocabulary

A Find the eight nouns, three verbs, and three adjectives in **bold** in "Economics—What's It All About?" Add them to the chart. Write them in the order they appear in the reading. Use the singular form of any plural noun. Use the base form of each verb.

	Nouns	Verbs	Adjectives	Other
1				
2				
	*			
3				
				since
5				
6				
7				
8				

*Include the article *the*.

 B Which words and phrases are new to you? Circle them here. Then find them in the reading. Look at the context. Can you guess the meaning?

Using the Target Vocabulary

 A   Complete these sentences **about the reading**. Use the words in the box.

debt	exchange	opportunity	scarce
economics	involves	property	the economy

1. _____ is the study of the ways that money, goods, and services are produced and used.

2. "The national _____" means all the money that a national government has borrowed from its own people and from foreign governments.

3. The phrase "_____" refers to the way that money, businesses, and products are organized in a particular local area, country, or other region.

4. Economist Pearl Claunch explains what an economist's point of view includes and affects. She explains what it _____.

5. Economists say we must make choices because everything of value is _____, meaning that it exists in a limited supply.

6. Because of your limited resources, when you choose to do or buy one thing, you generally lose the chance, or _____, to do or buy something else.

7. If someone's _____ lies in the way of a highway, that means the highway would cross that person's land.

8. Money makes it easier to _____ goods and services—to give one thing and get something else in return.

 B   These sentences are also **about the reading**. What is the meaning of each **boldfaced** word or phrase? Circle a, b, or c.

1. Some people worry that their country's national debt is on the **rise**. If there is a rise in something it is
   a. decreasing.   **b.** improving.   **c.** going up.

2. We all make our own **individual** decisions. *Individual* means
   a. separate from others.   **b.** volunteer.   **c.** emotional.

3. We have to make choices **since** we cannot have everything. *Since* means
   a. starting when.   **b.** in the past.   **c.** because.

4. Economist Pearl Claunch believes in a certain **approach** to decision making. *An approach to something* means
   a. a reason for doing it.   **b.** a method of doing it.   **c.** a result from doing it.

5. Whether you build a highway or a house, it involves **labor** and materials costs. *Labor* means
   a. time.   **b.** work.   **c.** taxes.

6. The government should **take** environmental costs **into account**. *Take something into account* means
   a. subtract it.   **b.** consider it.   **c.** raise it.

7. We may not all agree on which government actions are **necessary**. *Necessary* means
   a. needed.   **b.** modern.   **c.** complex.

DEVELOPING READING SKILLS

Cause and Effect

On a piece of paper, copy the start of each sentence, and then complete it using information from the reading. Try to paraphrase instead of quoting.

1. People may feel confused when they read or hear economic news because . . .

2. When we talk about the economy, we are talking about ourselves because . . .

3. Economist Pearl Claunch suggests using cost-benefit analysis because . . .

4. When planning a building project, government officials must consider more than just the costs of labor and materials because . . .

5. Governments create currency because . . .

6. People disagree on the role of the government in the economy because . . .

Understanding the Writer's Purpose

> To understand a reading, it is important to be aware of the writer's purpose—why he or she wrote the text. Consider these questions when reading or rereading:
> - Why did the writer include this particular information?
> - Why did the writer give the information in this order or in this particular way?

Circle a or b to complete the sentence with the writer's purpose.

1. The writer quotes economist Jim Stanford in the introduction . . .
   a. to make the reader feel the subject will not be hard to understand.
   b. to introduce some of the particular vocabulary that economists use.

2. The writer quotes economist Pearl Claunch . . .
   a. to introduce the different roles people play in the economy.
   b. to show how an economist thinks and looks at the world.

3. The writer mentions pizza and a movie . . .
   a. to give the reader some decision-making advice.
   b. to give the reader a real-world example of an economic idea.

4. The writer includes the last sentence . . .
   a. to remind the reader of Stanford's definition of economics.
   b. to show that no one agrees on what *economics* means.

EXPANDING VOCABULARY

New Contexts

A   Complete the sentences with the target words and phrases in the box. There are two extra words.

approach	economics	individual	opportunity	since
debt	exchange	labor	property	the economy

1. What's your _____ to learning new words?

2. The word "_____" can refer to land but also to anything you own.

3. The program gives foreign students the _____ to live with a French family.

4. _____ his injuries aren't serious, the doctors are letting the man go home.

5. A cake serves several people, while cupcakes are _____ servings.

6. Voters generally elect leaders whom they hope will be able to improve _____.

7. Ted served ten years in prison and feels that he has paid his _____ to society.

8. Barbara volunteers at Children's Hospital. Her work is a _____ of love.

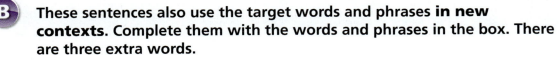

B   These sentences also use the target words and phrases **in new contexts**. Complete them with the words and phrases in the box. There are three extra words.

economics	individual	labor	rise	take into account
exchange	involve	necessary	scarce	the economy

1. _____ and history are two of the social sciences.

2. Can you _____ foreign money at any major bank?

3. Getting rid of chemical pesticides will _____ changes in farming methods.

4. I thought that was a required course, but it's not _____ after all.

5. When planning a road trip, it makes sense to _____ the weather, traffic, road conditions, and so on.

6. Wild bees have been disappearing and are now _____ in many places.

7. We should expect a _____ in home heating bills because of the increase in fuel costs.

Building on the Vocabulary: Word Grammar

The noun **economics** is a noncount noun. When *economics* is the subject of a verb, the verb is singular: *Economics **is** one of my favorite subjects.* The same is true of the nouns *mathematics, physics, politics,* and *news*.

The adjectives **economic** and **economical** have different meanings.

- *Economic* means "relating to economics and trade": *The country is heading for an **economic** crisis.*

- *Economical* means "using money or other resources carefully, without waste": *A smaller car is more **economical** because it can go farther on less fuel.*

The adverb form of both words is **economically**.

A Write three sentences. Use three of the noncount nouns in the box on page 220 as subjects.

1. _____
2. _____
3. _____

B Write two sentences. Use *economic* and *economical*.

1. _____
2. _____

Using New Words

Work with a partner. Choose five target words or phrases from the list on page 215. On a piece of paper, use each word or phrase in a sentence.

PUTTING IT ALL TOGETHER

Discussion

Talk with a partner and then with your whole class.

1. What is the opportunity cost of being a student?
2. On a piece of paper, do a cost-benefit analysis of studying English. Then compare yours with your partner's. What costs and benefits are the same for both of you? Which are different?

Writing

Choose a topic. Write a paragraph.

1. Describe the cost-benefit analysis you did for question 2 under **Discussion** above.
2. Think about decisions made by your national government on where to spend money (or not spend money). These decisions show what is most valued. Think of a specific way in which your personal values differ from the values expressed by the government in its decisions. Describe what you think your government should do differently.

CHAPTER 18

Behavioral Economics

How to decide?

GETTING READY TO READ

Read the statements and circle True or False. Then share your answers with a small group or your class and give examples.

1. I sometimes buy things I don't need.   True   False

2. Sometimes I make poor decisions about buying things.   True   False

3. "Two for the price of one" is always a good deal.   True   False

4. I'll usually say *yes* to something that's free.   True   False

5. Higher prices mean better quality.   True   False

Look at the words and definitions next to the reading. Then read without stopping.

Behavioral Economics

1   An economist sets up a table in a public place. Then he offers people walking by a choice of two chocolates. One is a gourmet[1] chocolate that he has priced at 15 cents, the other a smaller, more **ordinary** chocolate priced at just a penny.[2] More than 70 percent of the people who stop at the table prefer the higher-quality chocolate. **Even though** it costs 14 cents more, they are willing to pay the extra for it. Then the economist drops both prices by a penny, so the gourmet chocolate now costs just 14 cents, and the other one is free. All of a sudden, the numbers are reversed.[3] Now only 31 percent of the people who stop will pay 14 cents for the better chocolate. The other 69 percent go for the ordinary one—the free one.

2   Question: Why does the **thought** of getting something for free have such a strong effect on people's choices?

3   The same economist secretly visits some dormitories[4] at the U.S. university where he teaches, leaving a six-pack of soda in each of several shared refrigerators. In most cases, the sodas are gone within three days. The students have **helped themselves**. Then the economist returns, but this time, instead of a six-pack of sodas, he leaves a plate with six one-dollar bills. Three days later, all the money is still there.

4   Question: What made students decide to take a soda but not the money?

5   The economist and a team of researchers carry out a test that involves giving volunteers electric shocks. After one set of shocks, the volunteers get a pill that is supposed to make them feel less pain. They also get one of two brochures[5] about the pill. Some of the volunteers read that the pill they got is expensive, while others see that their pill has been marked down[6] to only 10 cents. None of the pills contains any **actual** pain reliever.[7] **Nevertheless**, when the volunteers **go through** another set of shocks after taking the pills, most of them report feeling less pain. Of the people who get the "high-priced medicine," almost everyone says that it helped. Of the people who get the "cheap medicine," only half say that it did.

6   Question: Why do people believe that a higher-priced pain reliever works better?

(continued)

[1] *gourmet* = relating to very good food and drink

[2] a *penny* = a U.S. coin worth $.01 or 1¢ (one cent)

[3] *reversed* = changed to the opposite of what they were

[4] a *dormitory* = a university building where students live

[5] a *brochure* = a thin book with information or advertising

[6] *marked down* = with the price lowered

[7] a *pain-reliever* = medicine that makes you feel less pain

7   For answers to these questions, read the work of Dan Ariely, the economist who handed out the chocolates and fake pills and visited those college dorms. Ariely is a professor of behavioral economics, a fairly new area of economics that has to do with economic decisions. He studies the **behavior** of consumers, borrowers, and investors.

8   According to the teachings of traditional economics, when people make economic decisions, we act in our own best interests. That is, most economists **assume** that we are **sensible** and will make the choices that do us the most good. What behavioral economists are finding, however, is that this is **frequently** not true: We often make poor economic choices. Our emotions get in the way of our calculations,[8] and we often repeat the same mistakes. Ariely calls people "predictably irrational" because our decisions often do not make sense and because he can predict the mistakes we will make.

[8] *calculations = work with numbers to figure out amounts or prices*

9   One thing that influences our decision making is the way that a choice is presented to us. According to Ariely, "Most people don't know what they want until they see it in context." We need to make **comparisons**. He uses an illustration like the one below to show that we cannot always trust those comparisons.

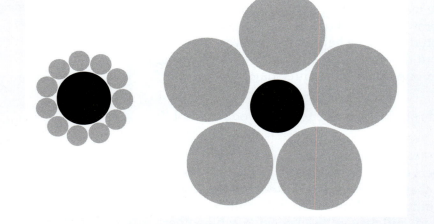

10   The two dark circles in the middle are the same size, but they do not seem to be, do they? The one on the right seems smaller because of the larger circles that **surround** it. Ariely says that this is exactly how our minds work. We see things—and people, experiences, and emotions—not as they are but **in relation to** others. When we are faced with certain choices, presented to us in

certain ways (for example, by smart salespeople), we are likely to make poor decisions.

11   Ariely hopes that as people learn more about when, where, and why we make poor decisions, we will understand ourselves better. Maybe we will learn to think differently. Nevertheless, even he **admits** to buying a thirty-thousand-dollar car—which was not the kind of car he truly needed—after learning that it came with three years of free oil changes.

The illustration is drawn from Ariely's book *Predictably Irrational*, New York: Harper, 2008.

Quick Comprehension Check

Read these sentences. Circle T (true) or F (false).

1. Behavioral economists study economic decision making.   T   F

2. Dan Ariely is a traditional economist.   T   F

3. Traditional economists expect people to know what's good for them.   T   F

4. Ariely does research that looks at people's choices.   T   F

5. Ariely says people often make the same kinds of mistakes.   T   F

6. Ariely has learned not to make poor consumer choices.   T   F

EXPLORING VOCABULARY

Thinking about the Target Vocabulary

 A   Find the three nouns, five verbs, and three adjectives in **bold** in "Behavioral Economics." Add them to the chart. Use the singular form of any plural noun. Use the base form of each verb.

	Nouns	Verbs	Adjectives	Other
1				
				even though
2				
3				
5				
				nevertheless
7				
8				
				frequently
9				
10				
				in relation to
11				

 B   Which words and phrases are new to you? Circle them here. Then find them in the reading. Look at the context. Can you guess the meaning?

Using the Target Vocabulary

 A Read each definition and look at the paragraph number. Look back at the reading on pages 223–225 to find the **boldfaced** word to match the definition. Write it in the chart.

Definition	Paragraph	Target Word
1. average or usual, not special or different	1	
2. real	5	
3. however	5	
4. showing good sense or judgment	8	
5. often	8	

B Complete these sentences **about the reading**. Use the words and phrases in the box.

admits	comparison	in relation to	thought
assume	even though	surround	went through
behavior	helped themselves		

1. People preferred the gourmet chocolates in spite of their higher price. _____ the price was higher, most people bought those.

2. People changed their minds when the one-cent chocolates became free. The idea, or the _____ , of getting something for nothing was very powerful.

3. The students did not wait for anyone to offer them a soda. They went ahead and took what they wanted. They _____.

4. The volunteers all experienced electric shocks. They _____ two sets of shocks, and in between, they took a pill.

5. Dan Ariely does research on how consumers, borrowers, and investors act. He studies their _____.

6. Traditional economists expect people to do cost/benefit analyses and make choices that are in our own best interests. They _____ that people will do this.

7. When you look at two things and compare them, you make a _____.

8. In the picture on page 224, you see two dark circles with other circles all around them. The other circles _____ the dark ones.

9. Ariely says that we do not look at things all by themselves. We compare them to other, similar things. We judge them _____ these other things.

10. Sometimes a person agrees that something is true but says it unwillingly. Ariely _____ that he made a bad decision buying a car. (He accepts the idea but isn't happy to say so.)

DEVELOPING READING SKILLS

Reading for Details

 Complete the chart with information from the first paragraph of "Behavioral Economics."

	Situation 1		Situation 2	
	Price	Percentage of Buyers	Price	Percentage of Buyers
Gourmet chocolate	15¢			
Ordinary chocolate	1¢			

 Reread the fifth paragraph. Number the steps in order from 1 to 6.

_____ a. The volunteers went through another set of shocks.

_____ b. Each volunteer read a brochure with information about their pill.

_____ c. The volunteers went through their first set of shocks.

_____ **d.** Each volunteer got a pill that he or she believed was a pain reliever.

_____ **e.** Volunteers agreed to take part in a test involving electric shocks.

_____ **f.** Many volunteers reported feeling less pain, including almost all of those who believed their pill was expensive.

C **Are these statements about the reading true or false? If the reading doesn't give the information, check (✔) *It doesn't say.***

	True	False	It doesn't say
1. Dan Ariely studies people's behavior in relation to economic decision making.	☐	☐	☐
2. All the people he studies know that they are part of his research.	☐	☐	☐
3. He uses volunteers for some of his research.	☐	☐	☐
4. He teaches traditional economics as well as behavioral economics.	☐	☐	☐
5. He sometimes studies the behavior of college students.	☐	☐	☐
6. He says consumers' emotions help them make sensible choices.	☐	☐	☐
7. He says making comparisons will keep consumers from making mistakes.	☐	☐	☐
8. He says getting something for free has a powerful influence on buying decisions.	☐	☐	☐

Summarizing

On a piece of paper, write a one-paragraph summary of "Behavioral Economics." Include answers to the following questions:

- Who is Dan Ariely?
- What is behavioral economics?
- What is one difference between Ariely's views and the teachings of traditional economics?
- According to Ariely, why should we learn more about our decision making?

If you wish, you can begin:

The reading "Behavioral Economics" introduces Dan Ariely, . . .

EXPANDING VOCABULARY

New Contexts

 These sentences use the target words and phrases **in new contexts**. What is the meaning of each **boldfaced** word or phrase? Circle a, b, or c.

1. **Help yourself to** the cookies. *Help yourself to something* means
   a. help me do it.
   b. don't expect my help.
   c. take whatever you want.

2. I hate the **thought** of carrying credit card debt from month to month. In this sentence, *thought* means
   a. a memory.
   b. an idea.
   c. a threat.

3. **Even though** they were expensive and she didn't need them, Joan bought the shoes. *Even though* means
   a. in spite of the fact that.
   b. because of the fact that.
   c. in addition to the fact that.

4. I don't know it for sure, but I **assume** that the story is true. *Assume* means
   a. take over.
   b. expect, believe.
   c. doubt.

5. Tom's parents were pleased with the teacher's report on his **behavior** in class. *Behavior* means

   a. grades.   **b.** relationships.   **c.** way of acting.

6. Poor Beth! She is **going through** a lot these days. In this sentence, *go through* means

   a. experience something upsetting.   **b.** spend a lot of money.   **c.** get rid of something.

7. The apartment has six rooms, but it's small **in relation to** the size of their family, since they have seven children. *In relation to* means

   a. in spite of.   **b.** in terms of.   **c.** in charge of.

B   **These sentences also use the target words in new contexts. Complete them with the words in the box. There are two extra words.**

actual	assume	frequently	ordinary	surround
admit	comparison	nevertheless	sensible	thought

1. The company is offering no security or benefits. _____, Leon has decided to take the job.

2. They say the project will cost one million, but everyone knows the _____ cost will be higher.

3. Engineers designing appropriate technologies are taking a _____ approach to the problems of developing countries.

4. A two-stroke engine pollutes so much that a four-stroke engine seems great by _____.

5. What started out as just another _____ day turned into the most exciting day of my life.

6. The man wouldn't _____ to being in the store until the police announced he had been caught on the security video.

7. Even though many people don't want to hear what he has to say, Jeff _____ speaks out on the effects of raising beef cattle.

8. Presidents who _____ themselves with "yes-men" are not open to considering new ideas or facing hard questions.

Building on the Vocabulary: Studying Collocations

Note the words used in phrases with the noun *comparison*.

The first test was so hard that the second seemed easy by comparison.

In comparison to/with burning oil, solar power offers many benefits.

I'd like to see a comparison of the two loans.

The speaker drew comparisons between the two approaches.

The new method is so much better than the old that there's no comparison (between them).

Complete the sentences. Write the preposition *between*, *by*, *of*, *to*, or *with*. There may be more than one answer in some cases.

1. A comparison _____ the two groups in the study showed similar results.

2. There is simply no comparison _____ the two companies in terms of productivity.

3. _____ comparison _____ much of the region, our local economy is strong.

4. The two economies are so different that it is impossible to draw any comparison _____ them.

Using New Words

Work with a partner. Choose five target words or phrases from the chart on page 226. On a piece of paper, use each word or phrase in a sentence.

PUTTING IT ALL TOGETHER

Discussion

Talk about these questions in a small group.

1. What did Ariely see in people's behavior when he offered people the choice of chocolates?

2. Why do you think the students took the sodas but not the money?

3. When you buy medicine, do you buy big-name brands (the kinds you see advertised on TV) or similar but cheaper "no-name" medicines? Why?

4. How much did Ariely pay for his car? How much did he save by getting three years of free oil changes?

5. What effect, if any, is this reading likely to have on your economic decision making? Why?

Writing

Choose a topic. Write a paragraph.

1. Write about question 3 or 5 from **Discussion** above.

2. Think of a time when you had to make an economic decision, such as whether or not to buy something, or which of two things to buy. Describe the choice you faced and how you made your decision.

CHAPTER 19

The Economics of Happiness

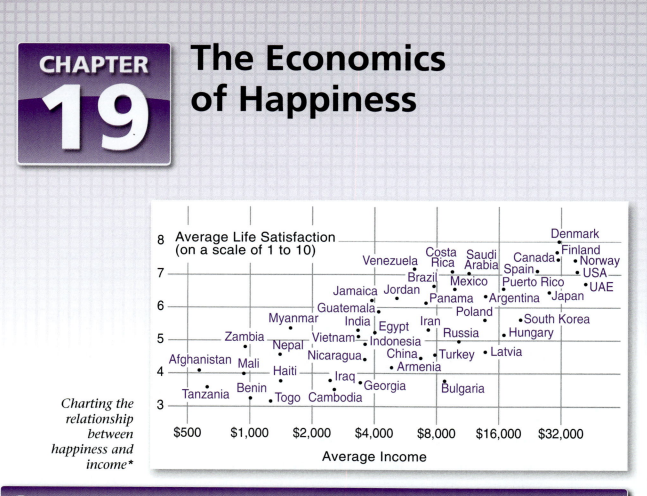

Charting the relationship between happiness and income*

GETTING READY TO READ

Talk about these questions with a partner.

1. Look at the graph above. Can you find your country? Is it where you would expect it to be in terms of average income? What about in terms of happiness?

2. Look at the countries at the top and at the bottom, by income and by happiness. Are there any surprises there?

* Source: Betsey Stevenson and Justin Wolfers, Wharton School at the University of Pennsylvania (USA)

READING

Look at the words and definitions next to the reading. Then read.

The Economics of Happiness

1   People often think of economists as focusing on money, production, and the cold, hard facts of what happens in the marketplace. It may therefore come as a surprise to think of an economist asking, "How happy are you?" However, some economists very much want to know.

2   Richard Easterlin is an economist who has studied national happiness for years. In 1974, he presented a new theory.[1] He said that a nation's economic **growth** does not always lead to its people becoming happier. Poor people do become happier when they get enough money for basic needs, but beyond that, he said, more money does not mean more happiness.

3   Easterlin pointed to Japan as an example. In the years following World War II, Japan experienced an economic boom,[2] one of the biggest in the history of the world. Between 1950 and 1970, its economic production grew by more than 600 percent. Japan grew from a country **torn apart** by war into one of the richest nations in the world. Surprisingly, however, the people of Japan did not seem to grow any happier. According to one **poll**, they actually felt less **satisfied** with their lives in the early 1970s than they had been fifteen years before. They were richer, yes, but happier, no.

4   For years, economists accepted Easterlin's theory. The public[3] accepted it, too. It fit in with the popular idea that money cannot buy happiness. Perhaps we want to believe in this idea because we all hope that happiness is within our reach even when **wealth** is not.

5   Easterlin's theory was back in the news in 2008. Two young economists, Betsey Stevenson and Justin Wolfers, **argued** against it in a paper that other economists found very interesting. Their **position** was that money is, in fact, likely to bring happiness. They based their argument on information that further polls had **revealed** over the thirty-four years since Easterlin's paper. They said, "Our key finding[4] is that income appears to be closely related to happiness. . . . Most countries get happier as they get wealthier, and wealthy countries have **citizens** with greater happiness than poor countries."

6   Some of their information came from the Gallup Organization, a well-known and respected polling **organization**, which found that people in the richest countries are happiest with their lives. At least one-third of the people in those countries give themselves

[1] a *theory* = an idea that explains why something happens

[2] a *boom* = a sudden increase in business activity

[3] *the public* = all the ordinary people

[4] a *finding* = a piece of information learned through research

a score of 8, 9, or 10 on a happiness **scale** of 1 to 10. The very rich and happy nation at the top of the list is Denmark. Denmark, along with Switzerland and Austria, also sits at the top of other lists by economists who do similar research. Who is at the bottom? Poor African nations, among them Tanzania, Togo, and Benin.

7   **As for** the case of postwar Japan:[5] Stevenson and Wolfers also looked back at the research done there. It turns out that the question in the poll changed over time. If you look only at the years in which the question stayed the same, then the percentage of people who **rated** themselves as "satisfied" or "completely satisfied" actually did rise.

8   The **central** idea, then, is that the economic growth of a nation does generally lead to more happiness for its citizens. In poor countries, it can mean better food and housing and more choices in life. In rich countries, it can pay for research and medical care that help people enjoy longer, healthier lives. Easterlin, however, remains unconvinced.[6] He notes that China and the United States both grew richer in recent years without growing any happier.

9   Easterlin, Stevenson, and Wolfers would all agree on at least one thing: Money is not the only factor[7] that influences happiness. Stevenson and Wolfers report that Latin American countries are happier than income alone would predict, and East European countries are less happy.

10   When Stevenson and Wolfers speak about income and its influence, they maintain that what matters is *absolute income*—how much you make in dollars, pesos, euros, or yen. Easterlin, on the other hand, believes that *relative income* matters more—how much you make in comparison with others. After your basic needs are met, you compare yourself with the people around you. How happy you are depends not on how much you have but on how much you still want.

11   Such comparisons may be human nature—or are they? Psychology[8] professor Sonja Lyubomirsky does not believe that happy people think this way. In her research, she has asked people who they compared themselves with. Less happy people, she reports, "went on and on." How did happier people **respond**? She says, "They didn't know what we were talking about."

[5] *postwar Japan* = Japan in the years after World War II

[6] *unconvinced* = not made to believe in someone's argument

[7] a *factor* = one of several things that cause or influence a situation

[8] *psychology* = the study of the mind and how it works

Stevenson and Wolfers's words come from "Q&A: Betsey Stevenson and Justin Wolfers: It turns out money really does buy happiness. Uh-oh.", by Daniel Akst, *Boston Sunday Globe*, November 23, 2008, C4. Sonja Lyubomirsky was quoted in "Can Money Buy Happiness?" by David Futrelle, CNNMoney.com, July 18, 2006. Retrieved January 5, 2009, from http://money.cnn.com/magazines/moneymag/moneymag_archive/2006/08/01/8382225/index.htm.

Quick Comprehension Check

Read these sentences. Circle T (true) or F (false).

1. Some economists measure national happiness.   T   F

2. National happiness depends entirely on economic
   growth.   T   F

3. Postwar Japan affected economists' thinking about
   happiness.   T   F

4. New information has come out about happiness in
   postwar Japan.   T   F

5. The role of income in happiness is well understood
   by all.   T   F

6. You can only be happy by comparing yourself to
   others.   T   F

EXPLORING VOCABULARY

Thinking about the Target Vocabulary

A **Find the seven nouns, five verbs, and two adjectives in bold in "The Economics of Happiness." Add them to the chart. Use the singular form of any plural noun. Use the base form of each verb.**

	Nouns	Verbs	Adjectives	Other
2				
3				
4				
5				

	Nouns	Verbs	Adjectives	Other
6				
7				as for
8				
11				

B Which words and phrases are new to you? Circle them here. Then find them in the reading. Look at the context. Can you guess the meaning?

Using the Target Vocabulary

A Complete these sentences **about the reading**. Use the words and phrases in the box.

argue	central	organization	rate	scale
as for	growth	poll	revealed	torn apart

1. In 1974, economist Richard Easterlin maintained that a growing national economy did not mean the people of that nation would become happier. He said economic _____ did not always lead to greater national happiness.

2. When a country has been _____ by war, it has been badly hurt and has many problems.

3. To find out what people in general think about something, you can take a _____. That means asking many people the same question.

4. When researchers _____ that something is true or should be done, they present what they believe with clear reasons for it.

5. We know more about economic growth and national happiness now than we did in the past. Polls taken around the world have _____ this information.

6. The writer suggests that we can trust the information from the polls because they were taken by a respected _____. This word refers to a group, sometimes a business, formed for a particular purpose.

7. Gallup pollsters asked people to rate themselves on a _____ of 1 to 10. Each number was a measure of happiness.

8. The writer raises the subject of Japan by saying, "_____ the case of postwar Japan, . . ." Use this phase to introduce a new but related topic.

9. When you give an opinion of yourself or apply a certain value to yourself, you _____ yourself.

10. When Stevenson and Wolfers speak about their "key finding," they are talking about the _____ idea from their research.

B These sentences are also **about the reading**. What is the meaning of each **boldfaced** word? Circle a, b, or c.

1. Many people in rich countries say they are **satisfied** with their lives. *Satisfied* means
   a. happy.
   b. confused.
   c. annoyed.

2. People often say that happiness does not depend on **wealth**. *Wealth* means
   a. your health and well-being.
   b. your personal development.
   c. how much money you have.

3. The economists mentioned in the reading have certain **positions** on the role of the economy in national happiness. Positions are
   a. resources.
   b. opinions.
   c. treatments.

4. Does a nation's economic growth make its **citizens** happier? Citizens are people who
   a. have the right to live in a country.
   b. are political leaders in a country.
   c. study the economy of a country.

5. Less happy people **responded** differently from happier people to questions about comparing themselves with others. *Respond* means
   a. blame.
   b. admit.
   c. answer.

DEVELOPING READING SKILLS

Text Organization

Number these events in chronological order from 1 (the first to happen) to 6 (the most recent).

_____ **a.** Easterlin presented his theory.

_____ **b.** Easterlin studied information from polls done in postwar Japan.

_____ **c.** Stevenson and Wolfers presented their theory.

_____ **d.** Stevenson and Wolfers studied thirty-four years' worth of polls.

_____ **e.** Economists accepted the idea that economic growth did not always mean greater happiness.

_____ **f.** Japan experienced an economic boom.

Understanding the Main Idea and Major Points

 Which statement gives the main idea of the reading? Check (✔) your answer.

☐ **1.** Economists disagree about the relationship between a country's economy and its citizens' happiness.

☐ **2.** Economists have finally agreed that national wealth is based on national happiness.

☐ **3.** Economists report that individual happiness depends on not comparing yourself with other people.

B   According to the reading, which researcher or researchers believe in each of the ideas below? In each column, write *yes* or *no* or put a question mark if the reading does not say.

	Easterlin	Stevenson and Wolfers	Lyubomirsky
1. Getting the money to meet basic needs makes poor people happier.			
2. When a country's economy grows, it does not mean that its citizens get happier.			
3. Most nations become happier as they get richer.			
4. Money is not the only thing that affects national happiness.			
5. A person's happiness depends on how much he has compared to others.			
6. Happy people don't usually compare themselves with others.			

EXPANDING VOCABULARY

New Contexts

A **Complete the sentences with the target words and phrases in the box. There are two extra words.**

argue	organization	rated	scales
central	polls	responded	torn apart
citizens	position	satisfied	wealth

1. The United Nations is an international _____.

2. _____ customers will bring repeat business.

3. Oil is the major source of the country's _____.

4. I've sent out at least ten party invitations, but no one has _____ yet.

5. Some economists _____ that we make decisions by making comparisons.

6. Protecting our natural resources is in the best interests of all our _____.

7. The _____ conflict in a story is the problem facing the main character.

8. Reporters asked the president to explain his _____ on the national debt.

9. _____ show that many voters have not yet made up their minds.

10. The country has been _____ by war for so long that thousands of children have grown up without ever attending school.

B **Read these sentences. Write the boldfaced target words or phrases next to their definitions. There is one extra definition. Put an X next to it.**

a. The X-ray **revealed** a break in the bone.

b. Almost 90 percent of the students **rated** the professor "excellent."

c. Bob has had a very successful career. **As for** his personal life, that is a different story.

d. The **growth** of modern technology has meant amazing changes in communications.

e. On a **scale** of 1 to 10, with 10 the worst pain you can imagine, how much pain are you currently feeling?

**Target Words
or Phrases**   **Definitions**

1. _____ = an increase in amount, size, or degree

2. _____ = showed something that had been hidden, secret, or unknown

3. _____ = a way to measure the force, speed, or amount of something

4. _____ = assumed something to be true without knowing for sure

5. _____ = used when you start talking about something new that is related to what you were talking about before

6. _____ = gave an opinion about the value or worth of someone or something

Building on the Vocabulary: Studying Collocations

> Certain prepositions often follow certain nouns, verbs, and adjectives.
>
> *Is he **arguing for** or **against** the plan?*
>
> *Your work has been **central to** the company's success.*
>
> *Anyone running for election must take **positions on** many issues.*
>
> *The company has not yet **responded to** my e-mail.*
>
> *Stores want customers to be **satisfied with** the service they receive.*

Choose three of the words from the box. Write a sentence using each one + a preposition.

1. _____

2. _____

3. _____

Using New Words

Work with a partner. Choose five target words or phrases from the chart on pages 237–238. On a piece of paper, use each word or phrase in a sentence.

PUTTING IT ALL TOGETHER

Discussion

Talk about these questions in a small group.

1. How would you answer the question "How satisfied are you with your life?" if the person asking the question were

   a. a pollster* on the street

   b. a family member

   c. your best friend

2. Are polls common in your country? Richard Easterlin wonders whether people from different cultures respond differently to polls. Perhaps age matters, too. What do you think?

* a *pollster* = a person who asks people questions as part of a poll

3. The three economists agree on at least one thing: Money is not the only thing that affects happiness. What examples do Stevenson and Wolfers give to support this idea? In your opinion, what else affects national happiness?

Writing

Choose a topic. Write a paragraph.

1. Choose one of the **Discussion** questions above.

2. Write about your country's wealth, in relation to other countries, and its happiness. What would make the citizens of your country happier?

3. Do you believe it is human nature to compare ourselves with others? How do you think that would affect a person's happiness?

CHAPTER 20

Muhammad Yunus and the Grameen Bank

Economist and Nobel Prize winner Muhammad Yunus

GETTING READY TO READ

Talk with a partner or with your class.

1. What are some reasons why people go to a bank to borrow money? Have you ever taken out a bank loan?

2. Why do banks lend money to some people and not to others? How do banks make money?

3. What do you know about the Nobel Prize?

READING

Look at the picture, words, and definitions next to the reading. Then read without stopping.

Muhammad Yunus and the Grameen Bank

1   In 1974, economist Muhammad Yunus lent about twenty-seven dollars of his own money to a group of poor women in a small **village** in Bangladesh. It was the first of his microloans—very small loans for people too poor to get money from traditional banks. From there, he went on to develop the Grameen Bank, whose purpose is to help the poor[1] make better lives for themselves. In 2006, Yunus and the Grameen Bank won a Nobel Prize, but it was not the prize for economics.

[1] *the poor* = poor people in general

2   Yunus was born in 1940 in the village of Bathua in Chittagong, then in British India, now in Bangladesh. He was the third of nine children, the son of a jeweler.[2] The family was wealthy enough for Yunus to get a good education in Bangladesh and the United States, where he earned a **degree** in economics in 1970.

[2] a *jeweler* = someone who makes and/or sells jewelry, gold, watches, etc.

3   Yunus was a professor of economics at Chittagong University in 1974 when he began his fight against **poverty**. He discovered that a very small loan could make a big difference in the life of a poor person. His first such loan went to women who made furniture out of bamboo[3] in the village of Jobra. The women had been getting loans from moneylenders[4] to buy the bamboo. They then sold the furniture to the moneylenders to pay back the loans. However, because the women had to pay extremely high rates of interest, their profits were too small to support their families. At the time, they had nowhere else to go for loans. Traditional banks, which offered **reasonable** interest rates, were not willing to make tiny loans. They were also not willing to deal with poor people, whom they considered bad risks (that is, unlikely to pay the money back).

[3] *bamboo*

[4] a *moneylender* = a person whose business is lending money

4   The Grameen Bank is different because its **chief** purpose is to help poor families help themselves. One of the unusual things about this bank is that it does not make borrowers sign **contracts**. **In effect**, it makes loans based on trust. In addition, its loans are not based on any collateral. *Collateral* means property that a bank can take if a borrower does not repay a loan. For example, when

(continued)

someone gets a bank loan to buy a house, if the borrower does not repay the money, the bank can take the house. The house is collateral for the loan.

5   Traditional banks are based on the idea that the more you have, the more you can borrow. If you have nothing, you can get nothing. The Grameen Bank exists to serve those who have nothing and focuses instead on a borrower's potential.[5] It also believes that the bank should go to the people rather than the people having to go to the bank. It has **staff** who go out into more than 80,000 villages spread out all over Bangladesh. Among its borrowers, about 95 percent are women. They use their loans to buy chickens or a cow, to plant a vegetable garden or some fruit trees, to make and sell clothing or other goods, or to start up some other kind of small business. They repay their loans in tiny, weekly amounts.

6   Grameen Bank is also unusual in that it requires each borrower to belong to a five-person *solidarity[6] group*. At first, only two members of the group may apply for loans. Depending on how well these two follow the rules and repay what they **owe**, the next two borrowers can apply, and finally, the fifth. Group members support one another's efforts, and peer pressure[7] helps keep individual **accounts** in order. The **system** is working, says Muhammad Yunus. In 2008, he wrote, "Grameen's repayment rates have averaged better than 98 percent."

7   The Grameen Bank has been a source of ideas and a **model** for many other organizations. It has proven that a bank can help people and make strong profits, too. Organizations dealing in microcredit now exist around the world, from Asian villages to poor **neighborhoods** in New York City. Yunus calls the Grameen Bank a good example of how businesses can deal with economic problems that are usually left to governments.

8   In 2006, when the Norwegian Nobel Committee gave a prize to Muhammad Yunus and the Grameen Bank, it was the Nobel Peace Prize. The committee **praised** their work in creating "economic and social development from below." It linked[8] their work to the effort to create world peace, saying that the world will never gain lasting peace unless large population groups find ways to **break out of** poverty. We now know microloans are one way, thanks to Muhammad Yunus and the Grameen Bank.

_____

Muhammmad Yunus's words come from his article "How Legal Steps Can Help to Pave the Way to Ending Poverty." Retrieved January 9, 2009, from http://muhammadyunus.org/content/view/166/127/lang,en/.

[5] *potential* = a natural ability that could turn into something good

[6] *solidarity* = loyalty among members of a group or between groups with the same goal

[7] *peer pressure* = a feeling that you must do as others in your group do to be accepted

[8] *linked* = connected

Quick Comprehension Check

Read these sentences. Circle T (true) or F (false).

1. Muhammad Yunus is an economist from Bangladesh.   T   F

2. Poor people always get the lowest interest rates.   T   F

3. The government in Bangladesh organized the Grameen Bank.   T   F

4. The bank makes loans to people that other banks will not serve.   T   F

5. Borrowers from the Grameen Bank have to work in groups.   T   F

6. Yunus won the Nobel Prize in Economics.   T   F

EXPLORING VOCABULARY

Thinking about the Target Vocabulary

 A Find the nine nouns, three verbs, and two adjectives in **bold** in "Muhammad Yunus and the Grameen Bank." Add them to the chart. Use the singular form of any plural noun. Use the base form of each verb.

	Nouns	Verbs	Adjectives	Other
1				
2				
3				
4				
				in effect

	Nouns	Verbs	Adjectives	Other
5				
6				
7				
8				

 B **Which words and phrases are new to you? Circle them here. Then find them in the reading. Look at the context. Can you guess the meaning?**

Using the Target Vocabulary

A **Read each definition and look at the paragraph number. Look back at the reading on pages 235–236 to find the boldfaced word or phrase to match the definition. Write it in the chart.**

Definition	Paragraph	Target Word or Phrase
1. legal written agreements between two people, businesses, etc., saying what each will do	4	
2. the people who work for an organization	5	
3. records of the money that a person or company takes in and pays out	6	
4. a perfect example of something good and therefore worth copying	7	
5. succeed in getting out of a place you don't want to be (like a prison)	8	

B Complete these sentences **about the reading.** Use the words and phrases in the box.

chief	in effect	owes	praised	system
degree	neighborhoods	poverty	reasonable	village

1. Muhammad Yunus made his first microloan to women living in a small _____ (a place too small to call a town).

2. He earned a _____ in economics by completing a university program.

3. Yunus became involved in helping people living in _____ (the situation of being very poor).

4. Moneylenders in Jobra charged interest rates that were neither fair nor sensible. Banks, however, charged _____ rates.

5. The most important goal of the Grameen Bank is helping the poor. That is its _____ purpose.

6. Most banks make a borrower sign papers. Then, if necessary, the bank can go to court to get its money back from the borrower. The Grameen Bank does not do this. _____, it makes loans based on trust.

7. After someone borrows money from the bank, he or she _____ this money to the bank and must repay it.

8. The Grameen Bank uses five-person solidarity groups as part of its _____—its way of organizing the work it does.

9. The system created by the Grameen Bank has been copied in other parts of the world, including small areas, or _____, of New York City.

10. The Nobel Prize Committee announced that Muhammad Yunus and the Grameen Bank had done excellent work. The Committee _____ their work.

DEVELOPING READING SKILLS

Understanding the Main Idea and Major Points

 A **Which statement expresses the main idea of the reading? Check (✔) your answer.**

☐ **1.** Muhammad Yunus is an economist from Bangladesh who won the Nobel Prize for Peace.

☐ **2.** Economist Muhammad Yunus developed the Grameen Bank to help the poor of Bangladesh get loans to improve their lives.

☐ **3.** The Grameen Bank is different from traditional banks in its purpose and its approach to lending money.

B **On a piece of paper, write at least one complete sentence to answer each question about a major point in the reading. Try to paraphrase; use quotations only if you must.**

1. Who is Muhammad Yunus?

2. What is the Grameen Bank?

3. Why did Muhammad Yunus and the Grameen Bank win the Nobel Prize for Peace?

Understanding Supporting Details

Complete the sentences with details from the reading.

1. In 1974, Yunus _____

_____

2. The women of Jobra _____

_____

3. Traditional banks don't make loans to the poor for two reasons:

_____

_____

4. The Grameen Bank is different from traditional banks in at least two ways: _____

_____

5. A solidarity group is _____

_____

EXPANDING VOCABULARY

New Contexts

A Complete the sentences with the target words and phrases in the box. There are two extra words.

accounts	contracts	model	praised	system
broke out	degrees	poverty	staff	village

1. "An economic _____" refers to all the parts of an economy that work together as a whole—labor, businesses, government, and so on.

2. What used to be a quiet fishing _____ has become a summer tourist attraction.

3. The U.S. president's chief of _____ is sometimes called the second most powerful person in Washington.

4. From a childhood in _____, she rose to become a highly successful businessperson.

5. Police are searching for two prisoners who _____ during the night.

6. The person who keeps the books for a business is in charge of keeping records of _____.

7. Some professional baseball players have _____ worth millions of dollars.

8. That college doesn't give _____ in business or computer science.

B These sentences also use the target words and phrases **in new contexts**. What is the meaning of each **boldfaced** word or phrase? Circle a, b, or c.

1. Anita **owes** me some money. *Owes* means
   a. wants to borrow.   b. needs to repay.   c. is offering.

2. Ellen's boss is her **chief** source of worry these days. *Chief* means
   a. main.   b. normal.   c. ordinary.

3. If everyone takes a **reasonable** approach to the discussion, I'm sure we can come to an agreement. *Reasonable* means
   a. right and true.   b. individual.   c. fair and sensible.

4. Parents are always happy when someone **praises** their children. *Praise someone* means
   a. make predictions about him/her.   b. say nice things about him/her.   c. respond to him/her.

5. They attend a school in their own **neighborhood**. *Neighborhood* means
   a. public property.   b. a small area of a town or city.   c. people who live near one another.

6. Paolo has a good **system** for reviewing new vocabulary. A system is
   a. a method.   b. a source.   c. technology.

7. I'm working fewer hours for the same money, so **in effect**, I got a raise. Use *in effect* to introduce
   a. the real situation.   b. an example.   c. a description of a crisis.

Building on the Vocabulary: Studying Collocations

Certain words go with the noun *degree*.

- You **get** or **earn a degree in** a subject. Then you **have** or **hold a degree (from** a school).

- A college or university **grants a degree to** or **confers a degree on** someone. (A high school grants a diploma.)

- There are many types of degrees, including **associate's, bachelor's, master's, doctoral,** and **honorary degrees.**

Complete the sentences.

1. I (have / want to earn) a degree _____

2. I (have / want) a/an _____ degree.

3. Many universities have _____ honorary degrees _____ Muhammad Yunus.

Using New Words

Work with a partner. Choose five target words or phrases from the list on pages 249–250. On a piece of paper, use each word or phrase in a sentence.

PUTTING IT ALL TOGETHER

Discussion

Talk about these questions in a small group.

1. How did Muhammad Yunus get started in his fight against poverty? Tell the story of the women of Jobra.

2. What is a solidarity group? What effect do the groups have on borrowers? Why do you think they have this effect?

3. Why do you think so many of the Grameen Bank's borrowers are women?

Writing

Choose a topic. Write a paragraph.

1. Many people respect and admire Muhammad Yunus for his work helping people break out of poverty. Who is someone you respect and admire? Write about that person, and explain what he or she has done to earn your respect.

2. For someone who is trying to break out of poverty, getting a microloan is only one step in a long process. Have you ever set a goal for yourself that required a long time and much work to reach? Explain your goal, and describe what you did or are doing to reach it.

UNIT 5 Wrap-up

 A Match words with similar meanings. Match 1–8 with a–h and 9–16 with i–p. Write the letters.

1. ____ actual   a. average   9. ____ reasonable   i. employees
2. ____ assume   b. personal   10. ____ respond   j. riches
3. ____ exchange   c. needed   11. ____ reveal   k. method
4. ____ frequently   d. real   12. ____ since   l. sensible
5. ____ individual   e. work   13. ____ staff   m. idea
6. ____ labor   f. often   14. ____ system   n. because
7. ____ necessary   g. trade   15. ____ thought   o. show
8. ____ ordinary   h. believe   16. ____ wealth   p. answer

 B Complete the sentences with the words and phrases in the box. There are two extra words or phrases.

admitted	even though	in relation to	satisfied
argued	helped themselves	owed	scale
as for	in effect	rose	took into account

1. I don't see them regularly _____ we live in the same building.
2. He's lucky—the cost of living there is low _____ his income.
3. Fuel costs _____ for the third month in a row.
4. Are you _____ with the services your school provides?
5. Jack put the pizza on the table and his brothers _____.

256

6. Ben was such a great help that I felt I _____ him something in return.

7. The tomatoes in the garden are doing well, but _____ the spinach, that's been less successful.

8. If the government is unwilling to spend any more money on the program, then _____, the program is over.

9. When the bank decided whether to give me a loan, it _____ my work history.

10. One economist _____ that the crisis could have been avoided, but most disagreed.

EXPANDING VOCABULARY

Use words from word families 1–6 to complete the sentences below. Use your dictionary if you have questions about word meanings.

	Nouns	Verbs	Adjectives	Adverbs
1	comparison	compare	comparable comparative	comparably comparatively
2	economics economist economy	economize	economic economical	economically
3	involvement	involve	involved	
4	praise	praise	praiseworthy	
5	response	respond	responsive	
6	surroundings	surround	surrounding	

1. **a.** The other job offers better benefits, but the pay is _____ to what I earn now.

   b. His house has only three rooms, but the other houses in the village have just two, so his is _____ large.

2. **a.** Pat decided to _____ by going out to eat less often.

   b. Poor countries need _____ development.

3. a. Schools do better when the children's parents get _____.

   b. The man admitted his _____ in the crime.

4. a. Yunus has received a great deal of _____ for his work.

   b. In spite of the manager's _____ efforts, the store failed.

5. a. The patient's condition is serious but _____ to treatment.

   b. I've been calling and calling but getting no _____.

6. a. "Your _____" is another way to say your immediate environment.

   b. The fire was so huge that police blocked off the _____ streets.

A PUZZLE

Complete the sentences with words you studied in Chapters 17–20. Write the words in the puzzle.

Across

2. I spent years repaying my loans until finally I was out of d_____.

4. If something interesting is s_____, it's often expensive.

6. Smith's approach to developing appropriate technologies can serve as a m_____.

7. The company keeps a close watch on its c_____ competitor.

9. They're open to a new a_____ to solving the problem.

10. He was dissatisfied with the contract. N_____, he signed it.

11. The g_____ of the business has brought rising profits.

Down

1. A psychologist studies people's thoughts, emotions, and
   b_____.

3. Signs of poverty are everywhere in the n_____.

4. Most people use the Celsius s_____ when measuring temperatures.

5. Beekeepers used to pay farmers to put beehives on their
   p_____.

8. I would r_____ that movie three stars out of a possible five.

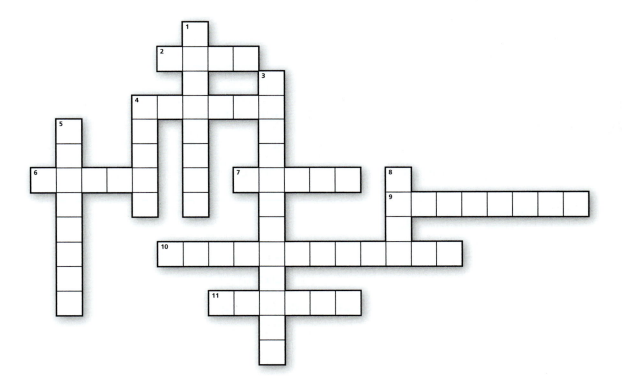

BUILDING DICTIONARY SKILLS

Phrasal verbs, like other verbs, can have more than one meaning. Look at the dictionary entries below. Then read each sentence and write the number of the meaning.

> **go through** *phr v*
> **1 go through** sth to have a very upsetting or difficult experience: *She's just gone through a divorce.*
> **2 go through** sth to use all of something: *Jeremy goes through at least a quart of milk every day!*
> **3** if a deal, agreement or law goes through, it is officially accepted: *My car loan has finally gone through.*
> **4 go through** sth to look at, read, or explain something carefully: *She had to go through all her uncle's papers after he died.*
>
> **go through with** sth *phr v* to do something you had planned or promised to do: *I'm not sure if I can go through with the wedding.*

1. _____ **a.** Runners go through shoes quickly.

   _____ **b.** Pam has been going through a lot since she lost her job.

   _____ **c.** We have a contract—the deal went through yesterday.

   _____ **d.** Get a lawyer to go though the contract with you.

> **break•out**[1] /ˈbreɪkaʊt/ *adv* successful, and making someone or something famous or popular: *a breakout performance by Williamson*
> **breakout**[2] *n* [C] an escape from a prison

2. _____ **a.** No prisoner has ever broken out of there.

   _____ **b.** The war broke out sixteen years ago.

   _____ **c.** Breaking out of poverty is hard.

   _____ **d.** Pat's face broke out on the day for school photos.

> **tear apart** *phr v* **1 tear** sth ⟺ **apart** to make a group, organization, etc. start having problems: *Scandal is tearing the government apart.* **2 tear** sb **apart** to make someone feel extremely unhappy or upset: *It tore me apart to see her leave.*

3. _____ **a.** It tears me apart to see you so unhappy.

   _____ **b.** Their competition for power is tearing the organization apart.

Circle the letter of the word or phrase that best completes each sentence.

Example:

The United Nations is an international _____ with about 200 members.

a. competition **(b.)** organization **c.** population **d.** development

1. Only _____ can vote in a national election.
   a. clients **b.** villages **c.** citizens **d.** models

2. An island is an area of land _____ by water.
   a. torn apart **b.** surrounded **c.** set up **d.** taken over

3. In a situation like this, I think the _____ thing to do is to see a lawyer.
   a. confused **b.** uncertain **c.** recent **d.** sensible

4. The operation will _____ a team of doctors and nurses.
   a. attend **b.** involve **c.** attach **d.** respond

5. I _____ to call her, but I forgot.
   a. helped myself **b.** predicted **c.** meant **d.** spoke out

6. It is a very _____ problem with no easy solution possible.
   a. complex **b.** valuable **c.** plain **d.** economic

7. The fish became so _____ that environmental groups called on the government to protect it.
   a. scarce **b.** individual **c.** artificial **d.** renewable

8. The organization needs to raise a lot more money to reach its goal, but the officers think they will _____.
   a. keep up with it **b.** fill it out **c.** go through it **d.** make it

32. I need a better _____ for organizing my study time.

    a. scale   **b.** system   **c.** association   **d.** quality

33. Monday is Independence Day. _____, all government offices will be closed.

    a. While   **b.** At least   **c.** Therefore   **d.** Yet

34. I didn't mention the meeting because I _____ you already knew about it.

    a. occurred   **b.** earned   **c.** appeared   **d.** assumed

35. He can't _____ his problems by closing his eyes to them.

    a. estimate   **b.** improve   **c.** block   **d.** solve

36. The hospital _____ was not prepared to deal with such a number of injuries.

    a. staff   **b.** wealth   **c.** crisis   **d.** demand

37. It's best to _____ driving in the city during the busiest hours of the day.

    a. avoid   **b.** deserve   **c.** trade   **d.** design

38. Several economists _____ that the cost/benefit analyses were incomplete.

    a. exchanged   **b.** differed   **c.** argued   **d.** blamed

39. I don't believe Barbara would take such a big risk—it's just not in her _____ to do a thing like that.

    a. poll   **b.** nature   **c.** property   **d.** neighborhood

40. Has any other sport _____ so far and wide as soccer?

    a. gained   **b.** proven   **c.** blown   **d.** spread

See the Answer Key on page 266.

Vocabulary Self-Tests Answer Key

Below are the answers to the Vocabulary Self-Tests. Check your answers, and then review any words you did not remember. You can look up the word in the Index to Target Vocabulary on pages 267–268. Then go back to the reading and exercises to find the word. Use your dictionary as needed.

Vocabulary Self-Test 1, Units 1–2 (pages 104–106)

1. **b.** goods
2. **d.** drove
3. **c.** fair
4. **a.** as long as
5. **c.** nature
6. **c.** mean
7. **b.** had something to do with
8. **a.** break the habit
9. **d.** actually
10. **b.** right
11. **c.** willing
12. **a.** make it
13. **c.** process
14. **d.** situation
15. **b.** avoid
16. **a.** particular
17. **d.** so far
18. **d.** view
19. **b.** plain
20. **c.** spread
21. **b.** provides
22. **a.** demand
23. **a.** likely
24. **c.** attached
25. **d.** developments
26. **d.** are blocking
27. **b.** regularly
28. **a.** exist

Vocabulary Self-Test 2, Units 3–4 (pages 208–210)

1. **b.** sources
2. **b.** occurred
3. **d.** Urban
4. **c.** ink
5. **a.** attend
6. **c.** events
7. **a.** in spite of
8. **d.** resources
9. **c.** drip
10. **d.** criminal
11. **a.** annoyed
12. **b.** descriptions
13. **a.** blamed
14. **b.** estimating
15. **c.** imagination
16. **d.** society
17. **b.** accurate
18. **a.** make fun of
19. **c.** outer space
20. **d.** set out
21. **a.** yet
22. **a.** benefit
23. **b.** scientific
24. **d.** models
25. **c.** matters
26. **c.** production
27. **b.** Environmental
28. **a.** be better off

Vocabulary Self-Test 3, Units 1–5 (pages 261–264)

1. **c.** citizens
2. **b.** surrounded
3. **d.** sensible
4. **b.** involve
5. **c.** meant
6. **a.** complex
7. **a.** scarce
8. **d.** make it
9. **a.** even though
10. **d.** actual
11. **a.** conflict
12. **b.** reveal
13. **c.** as long as
14. **a.** in relation to
15. **d.** maintain it
16. **a.** chief
17. **c.** expert
18. **b.** position
19. **c.** lie
20. **a.** appropriate
21. **b.** threat
22. **c.** admitted
23. **c.** unless
24. **b.** Nevertheless
25. **d.** owed
26. **d.** so far
27. **b.** ordinary
28. **a.** process
29. **d.** views
30. **a.** model
31. **b.** varies
32. **b.** system
33. **c.** Therefore
34. **d.** assumed
35. **d.** solve
36. **a.** staff
37. **a.** avoid
38. **c.** argued
39. **b.** nature
40. **d.** spread

INDEX TO TARGET VOCABULARY